The Pastor's Guide *to* Personal Spiritual Formation

William Willimon, M. Robert Mulholland Jr., Steve Harper,
Marjorie J. Thompson, Bill Hybels, Reginald Johnson,
John David Walt, Jan Johnson, Neil B. Wiseman,
Douglas S. Hardy, Morris A. Weigelt, E. Dee Freeborn

Beacon Hill Press of Kansas City
Kansas City, Missouri

Library of Congress Cataloging-in-Publication Data

The pastor's guide to personal spiritual formation / William Willimon . . . [et al.].
    p. cm.
  ISBN 0-8341-2209-X (pbk.)
  1. Clergy—Religious life. 2. Spiritual formation. 3. Spiritual life—Christianity. 4. Pastoral theology. I. Willimon, William, 1946-

  BV4011.6.P37 2005
  248.8'92—dc22

                                                                    2005002555

10 9 8 7 6 5 4 3 2 1

Contents

Introduction

It's no secret that Scripture urges all believers to be "conformed to the image of" Christ, "transformed by the renewing of [the] mind," and changed "from glory to glory" (Rom. 8:29; 12:2; 2 Cor. 3:18, NASB). As a pastor, the mystery you face is more likely how you are supposed to fit this life of transformation into your own already strained lifestyle. Preaching, teaching, counseling, unexpected celebrations and tragedies—all seem to chew away at your time and energy. Little is left over to engage in the recommended pathways to spiritual refreshment and growth. Yet this is not unlike the dilemma confronting Christians in other occupations. Their resources are also worn and drained. They need someone to model how to live a life of renewal amid all the chaos. This is often one of the roles you fill as a pastor. After all, if you are too taxed to advance further on the transformational trail, what hope is there for your parishioners?

One way to resolve this is to broaden and deepen how you understand the "recommended pathways." You may discover that these spiritual disciplines, practices, means of grace—however you designate them—are more flexible and diverse than you first thought. *The Pastor's Guide to Personal Spiritual Formation* explores the rich variety and grace-laden freedom a formational lifestyle can bring. The writer of each chapter is thoroughly versed in the devotional life through experience and training. Together these writings look at both traditional and not-so-traditional practices. Some show you how to tailor the more familiar disciplines to fit the unique challenges of your personal lifestyle and ministry; others envision how ordinary activities can be pathways to extraordinary encounters with God. As a whole, this book demonstrates that a hectic lifestyle can transcend being an obstacle to practicing spiritual disciplines; it can instead become a spiritual discipline itself.

Read through these essays and drink from their wisdom. Allow the writers to mentor you in prayer, meditative reading, spiritual direction, and other acts of devotion. Let the authors introduce you to the wondrous freedom a life of spiritual formation brings as you explore the many ways we can touch and be touched by God. After a while, you may find yourself not only progressing along a spiritually invigorating path but also wooing your people to do the same.

Steve Harper, Ph.D., is the vice president of the Florida campus of Asbury Theological Seminary and professor of spiritual formation. Prior to assuming his current position in 1998, Dr. Harper was the director of The Pathways Initiative and dean of The Upper Room chapel. As director of The Pathways Initiative, Dr. Harper headed this new venture at The Upper Room to resource and support spiritual leaders and promote spiritual formation in the congregation. From 1980 to 1993, Dr. Harper taught at Asbury as a professor of spiritual formation and Wesley studies. In 1993 Dr. Harper and his wife, Jeannie, founded Shepherd's Care, an organization developed to minister to ministers. He has also served as executive director of A Foundation for Theological Education (AFTE).

Dr. Harper, an elder in the United Methodist Church's Florida Conference, is the author of numerous magazine articles and has written 12 books, including *John Wesley's Message for Today* (Zondervan, 1983), *Devotional Life in the Wesleyan Tradition* (Upper Room, 1983), *Praying Through the Lord's Prayer* (Upper Room, 1992), and *Devotional Life in the Wesleyan Tradition: A Workbook* (Upper Room, 1995).

Dr. Harper and Jeannie are the parents of two grown children, John and Katrina, and two grandchildren, Zoe and Isaac.

1

A Pastor's Approach to Spiritual Formation

Steve Harper

🍂 HE STAYED BEHIND DURING A BREAK TO VISIT WITH ME. I WAS leading a seminar on the spiritual life of the minister at a pastor's conference. I could tell by the look in his eyes that our conversation was going to be significant. He wasted no time in describing a mounting discouragement in his life and work. The tone of his story was familiar, as were a number of details. But he took me by surprise when he described his dilemma in these words, "Steve, I know what to do; I just don't want to do it anymore."

In that moment, the Spirit spoke to my spirit with this idea, "Steve, pay attention to what he just said. It is a thumbnail sketch of the ministerial crisis taking place in thousands of pastors today." Right before my eyes was a young man in ordained ministry, moving just beyond a decade of faithful service, describing a downward spiral of passion regarding his call. He was telling me that the crisis is not essentially one of skill; it is one of spirit. We know what to do; we just don't want to do it anymore.

Our approach to spiritual formation as pastoral leaders must begin here. Even though we all learn along the way where and how we need to sharpen and improve our "doing," we confront a deeper need—how to be and remain healthy in our "being." In that regard, we discover a disproportionate number of resources in the skill-based area but not so many in the spirit-based one. As one pastor told me, "Each week I receive mailings telling me how to have a better ministry, but precious few telling me how to be a better minister."

Without diminishing the connection between skill and spirit, this chapter will focus on the second area. I am writing for those who know what to do but find it increasingly difficult to want to do it. In this chapter I will seek to provide an overview of key attitudes and actions that will help us "restore the joy of our salvation" and the fulfillment of our calling. I have discovered these elements in Mark 3:13-19, the description of Jesus' invitation to the Twelve to join Him. I have found great solace and guidance in putting myself into this picture, and I want to invite you to do the same.

I have no priority order in mind in this exploration. You will need to arrange these things to best suit your ongoing formation. Some may already be in good shape. Some may be missing. And as you use this chapter to ponder your condition, other things besides these may arise for your consideration. But surely the following ingredients will be found in our lives as we seek to be pastoral leaders for the church.[1]

CONFIDENCE

Salvation means "wholeness," not merely going to heaven when we die. God has acted in Jesus Christ to save us, not exclusively for eternity, but also in time. Jesus said He came to give us "abundant life" (see John 10:10), and that means what our predecessors have called "the life of God in the human soul." One of the chief evidences of this life is a sense of confidence.[2]

I am surprised at how many pastors lack confidence. They approach their lives and their work more as employees than as beloved sons and daughters. The most extended and deep period of spiritual dryness I have ever experienced occurred when I lost this sense in my own life and settled for a kind of "mechanical" faithfulness. The recovery of an authentic and vital spirituality depended on a renewed sense that I was God's beloved. Brennan Manning writes about this in his book *The Rabbi's Heartbeat*:

> The recovery of passion begins with the recovery of my true self as the beloved. If I find Christ, I will find myself, and if I find my true self, I will find Him. This is the goal and purpose of our lives. John did not believe that Jesus was the most important thing; he believed that Jesus was the *only* thing.
>
> If John were to be asked, "What is your primary identity, your most coherent sense of yourself?" he would not reply, "I am a disciple, an apostle, an evangelist," but "I am the one Jesus loves."[3]

Brennan goes on to write about the multiple things that occur if we lack this fundamental quality in our lives—one of the greatest he feels is that we shift our sense of self from God and begin to try and find it in the approval of others, a no-win situation as far as he is concerned.

How does this happen? There is no single cause or simple way to describe our loss of confidence in the space of one chapter. But I believe it flows fundamentally from a graceless theology—one rooted in performance, whose voice keeps trying to convince us, "You are worth only as much as you do; valuable only as long as you produce; in my will only as you succeed." These impressions are deadly to our spiritual life. They rob us of a healthy core identity that is necessary for us to move out to do ministry in

Jesus' name. I think Jesus knew this, and that's why Mark could write about the Lord's invitation using the words "those whom he wanted" (3:13, NRSV). We are not all invited in the same way, but we are all wanted. That is an incredible idea, especially when we are prone to compare ourselves with others and feel inadequate. But we are God's beloved, and that is the bedrock of our spiritual formation.[4]

CALLING

In Mark 3:13, we also learn that Jesus "called to him" those whom He wanted. Following close on the heels of God's amazing love for us and our confidence that we are God's beloved, we find that we are called to become personally involved in the work of God upon the earth. I am told that Frank Laubach, pioneer missionary and father of the modern literacy movement, began each day with this prayer, "God, what are You doing in the world today that I can help You with?" Laubach understood that the spiritual life is the "vocational" life.

I like the word "vocation" and feel it needs to be recovered in our time, when the professionalization of ministry has often eclipsed it. Vocation comes from the Latin word *vocatio*. It means that another is speaking, and we are listening. Another is in control—leading, guiding, guarding, and blessing. We are taking our cues from a source outside of ourselves— from Christ, through the Holy Spirit. Our calling begins in God's universal call to salvation, finds expression in the general call to discipleship, and becomes focused in our particular call to ministry. But from start to finish, it is all about vocation.

I would like to tell you that it is possible to live "in the center of your calling" all the time, but you know I cannot do that. All of us must function at times and in ways that do not reflect our greatest strengths. Ministry is a generalist vocation. But just as concentric circles are not the center yet remain in relation to the center, we must live our lives and practice our ministries with our "call" as a primary point of reference. Without that core, ministry can become what one pastor described to me as "the never-ending round of feverish activity." In my own experience I call it being in touch with the "whats" of my ministry, but becoming a stranger to the "why."

No matter where you are, you can live vocationally. You can express your gifts and graces in some way. Obviously, the challenge is to do that to the greatest extent possible. And when doing so becomes more inhibited than permitted, God may be awakening in you the knowledge that a change is in order. But the good news is this—moving from one particular ministry expression to another does not change the *nature* of your calling, only the function and possibly the place. Our call is rooted in what I earlier described as the universal call to salvation and the general call to discipleship. As long as we dwell in those dimensions, we are free to allow God to use our lives in many different ways.

COMMUNION

Mark moves quickly to the nature of Jesus' call to the Twelve. He shows that the Master's first desire was that they be "with him." At the heart of the relationship was communion. In this original experience He was laying down the pattern that He wants to have with all of us who respond to His call. More than anything else, Christ wants to establish and maintain His relationship with us on the basis of deep and personal interaction.

I would immediately note that this is what Christian leaders also want at the deepest level of their lives. Too many of us have settled for "religious employment," when our hearts are breaking for rich fellowship. Chuck Swindoll has rightly noted that those he knows (himself included) are saying, "What we long for is to become more deeply and intimately acquainted with Christ."[5]

We are never nearer to the core of our spiritual formation than when we seek to personalize what it means to live "in Christ" and to have Christ "live in us."[6] Paul made no bones about it. He called such communion the great mystery: "Christ in you, the hope of glory" (Col. 1:27). But as he also pointed out, this kind of spiritual life is no longer hidden; Jesus came to reveal it. It is rooted in the profound communion that existed between Him and the Father, and it is reflected in the defining picture of what a Christ-disciple relationship is supposed to be. He spent the entirety of John 15 explaining it under the idea "abide in me as I abide in you" (v. 4, NRSV). And lest they (or we) miss the significance of this, twice He said, "Apart from me you can do nothing" (v. 5, NRSV).

I have spent my vocational years mostly in theological education. I believe in an educated clergy. But I am also frightened at how easily this can turn into self-reliance. We can substitute professional activities for personal intimacy. We begin to believe we can "master divinity" when instead it is our Lord's goal that we be mastered by divinity. In essence, we have joined the ancient and modern ranks of those for whom "acedia" (spiritual erosion and boredom) is the result. I have lost count of the number of clergy who have intersected my life in precisely that debilitating condition, and I am sorry for how often I have either flirted with or lived in it myself.

Brennan Manning's view sums it up: "One's personal relationship with Christ towers over every other consideration. What establishes preeminence in the Christian community is not office, title, or territory, not the charismatic gifts of tongues, healing, or inspired preaching, but only our response to Jesus' question, 'Do you love Me?'"[7] I cannot urge you strongly enough to heed this section and pay careful attention to Manning's words.

Guard your devotional life. Do not give away the time you should be giving to God. No matter when that time is in the day, or what term you use to describe it, be sure it is there. This does not "guarantee" authentic spirituality, and you will have your share of days when nothing seems to be happening. But the element of communion is that quality of our formation, without which we will surely die, and that quality that cannot be made up for by any other means.

We are to adopt a contemplative disposition in our ministry. For a long time I shied away from the word "contemplation." It sounded too passive and unusual. The computer age redeemed the term for me. Built into every computer are a number of "templates." They are the predetermined forms and formats that will help us do quality work. Thus to be a "contemplative" is to be "with the template." Jesus is our "template," and to the extent that we position ourselves close to Him, listen to His words, and follow His example, we will be contemplative pastors.[8]

COMMISSION

I grew up in an expression of Christianity that emphasized the Great Commission (Matt. 28:16-20). I believed it then, and I believe it now. But what I mistakenly thought for a long time was that the Great Commission came at the end of Jesus' ministry. In fact, it came at the beginning, right in our focal passage, when Jesus says that after being with Him, they were "to be sent out to proclaim the message, and to have authority to cast out demons" (Mark 3:14-15, NRSV). After His resurrection, Jesus had to regather the disciples and renew the mission, so naturally, the Great Commission was there—and there with a global significance they had not seen before. But what I want you to see in this chapter is that this ingredient itself was at the start and at the heart of their formation. In fact, this is both explicit and implicit in the name He gave to the Twelve: "apostles," or "those who are sent out." Their coming together would have lost its significance unless they had known from the beginning what being "with him" was leading to.

My favorite Bible verse is 2 Cor. 5:17: "If anyone is in Christ, there is a new creation: everything old has passed away; see, everything has become new" (NRSV). In many ways, I believe it is a power-packed summary of the Christian life, rooted in the very essence of communion we set forth in the previous section. But it fails to reach its intended mark without the words that follow: "All this is from God, who reconciled us to himself through Christ, and has given us the ministry of reconciliation" (v. 18, NRSV).

There is no separation or two-staged process in moving from communion to commission. As you may already know, the term "obey" comes from the Latin root that means "to listen." We discern and practice the ministry of reconciliation out of a deep, prior "listening" to God through Christ. For the apostles, it was an audible word, but also one that connected them to the written revelation of the Old Testament scriptures. Even more, it was the Incarnate Word, Jesus, who demonstrated how His own deep, prior "listening" enabled Him to practice ministries of compassion every day of His life.

A number of years ago, I discovered the difference between Christ's "works" and His "work." The Gospels are saturated with His many "works," but Jesus himself is aware that prior to and deeper than any specific action, there was a fundamental "work." That singular endeavor was to do only what the Father told Him to do.[9] His days were hectic (see Mark 6:31), and they called for many specific "works," but His aim was that all of His actions would flow from and be connected to His "work"—His attentiveness to the Father and His intention only to do the Father's will. And as with the Great Commission, I came to see that Gethsemane was not His first time to pray "not my will, but yours be done" (Luke 22:42); He had been praying that prayer every day of His life.

I have a friend who came to see how inseparably communion and commission are supposed to be. He discovered it at Wounded Knee, where he was protesting the mistreatment of Native Americans. He would have quickly told you that his was a "ministry of reconciliation," and he had spent years of his life devoted to this cause and all the ways it was (and still is) needed. But at Wounded Knee, he "gave out." He had nothing else to give, and in that crisis of faith (and physical stamina), he was able to hear something God had been trying to tell him for a long time. God called him to root his "works" in a prior and deeper "work." The effects were transformative. His ministry became truly that of the Great Commission, and his ministries of compassion found an expression they had never known before.

Some of you reading this chapter will need to come to your own "Wounded Knee." You will need to find that prior and deeper place, out of which all service emerges. You will discover that supernatural tasks require supernatural power. But others of you will need to read this section from the other end—namely, that the deep and prior "work" (contemplation in communion) is never an end in itself, and that it must emerge in what spiritual-formation language calls "social holiness." But however you come to it, the ingredient of commission (sent-out service in Jesus' name) will be a life-giving aspect of your approach to spiritual formation.

COURAGE

Woven into both the text and the definition of pastoral formation that I am emphasizing is the element of courage. Do we even have to comment on the fact that the two acts of "proclaiming the message" and "casting out demons" were charged with controversy and required great courage on the part of Jesus and His disciples? He was giving them an assignment that would cost Him His life, and many of theirs as well. He was inviting them into a ministry of courage.

What does it take to proclaim a message that people either have no desire to hear, or who respond negatively when they hear it, or both? What does it take to cast out demons—those that people would like to get rid of and some they would prefer to hold on to? It takes courage. There are dimensions of this right here in the United States, despite the fact that Christianity is usually socially acceptable—that is, it has a generally safe place in our cities and towns. But our brothers and sisters in other parts of the world can quickly and easily testify to the courage required to be faithful in their cultures.

A pastoral approach to spiritual formation must continually engage in the assessment of courage and what is required of us to fulfill the twin mandates of Kingdom proclamation and demonic deliverance. As far back as the fourth century A.D., John Chrysostom was declaring ministry to be a "dangerous vocation." I'm afraid we do not sufficiently communicate that idea in our seminaries and Bible colleges; thus we send out person after person with the erroneous belief that our faithful efforts will be met by a generous affirmation. It has never been so, and it will not be so in the future.

For a long time, I have been telling seminarians and pastoral leaders, "If you decide to take spiritual formation seriously, prepare to be misunderstood." It is impossible to predict where you will be misunderstood. I have seen it come from almost everywhere: the community in which we serve, the congregation itself, pastoral colleagues, and sometimes even judicatory leaders. Without trying to give you a complex, I can assure you that you will share in the sufferings of Christ if you order your life formationally. Courage is not always affirmed or rewarded, but it is the apostolic way. There is an inescapable call to engage in "prophetic ministry."[10]

If we take the formational paradigm of Mark 3:13-19 seriously, we will continue to see that this kind of courage is fueled not only by the recognition of massive human need in the areas of message and deliverance but also by remaining in deep communion with Christ who reveals His heart and will to us regarding these things. And I believe that ultimately our courage comes from knowing we are doing *His* will, not merely our own. And perhaps even deeper than that, it will emerge from the first point of this chapter—from the confidence that we are God's beloved sons and daughters, who have been called to identify God's will and lead others to follow it.

COMMUNITY

If it is not clear by now, it is time for me to say it directly—these elements of a pastoral approach to formation are connected. Just as Mark 3:13-19 is a unit, I believe the elements I'm describing exist together. To be sure, they may receive differing weights at different times and for different reasons. But to eliminate any is to weaken them all. And that is surely true in this new point regarding community. In both terms and tone, this passage is about plurality, not individuality.[11]

Without minimizing anything I've said thus far, and running the risk of even appearing to contradict myself in this chapter, let me say I am persuaded that for some of us, this may be the great need in our formation. Too much pastoral leadership is rooted in an unhealthy individualism and isolation. We have too many Lone Rangers building their kingdoms—too many leaders who believe that to be visionary means they alone have the vision. This must stop. We serve a Master who never acted apart from either a sense of God's presence or a connection to community. We follow a Christ who even asked on one occasion, "Why do you call me good?" (Luke 18:19) and lived every day with a clear and healthy humility. There is no valid ministry apart from this.

John Stott has written powerfully about this: "Too many behave as if they believed not in the priesthood of all believers but in the papacy of all pastors. Our model of leadership is often shaped more by culture than by Christ."[12] Unfortunately, that model is one too often deficient in community and too frequently defined by an unhealthy individualism that robs pastoral ministry of its humility and gentleness.

Where this community does not exist, I believe we are near the time when we should require it in some form—even though I am not ignorant or unconcerned about the "down sides" of doing this. But as you read this chapter, you have an option. You have the option to live in community. You do not have to chafe under an imposed rule to do it; you can create it with colleagues within and/or outside of your particular denomination or parachurch organization. I have seen it take all sorts of forms: prayer groups, spiritual direction, sermon study, continuing education, accountability covenants, and so on. I have seen leaders engage in community right in their own location. I have seen them form supportive community with colleagues far away through annual retreats together, monthly gatherings, Internet chats, and telephone conference calls. The point is simply that these leaders became convinced they could not live apart from community. And neither can you. Even our monastic brothers and sisters discovered that the hermetical life had to be cenobitic if it was to survive and thrive.[13]

COLLABORATION

Years ago, I met a person who bluntly told me, "God doesn't need me. God can do anything He wants to do." He spoke these words out of a deep depression, perhaps even despair. So I did not engage him in a theological debate but rather attempted to give him some pastoral care. But I believe both his spirit and his theology were wrong. To be sure, he needed a fresh infusion of life and hope, but he also needed to see what E. M. Bounds recognized nearly a hundred years ago, "People are his method." In a way we will never completely understand, God's power is most often expressed through human agency. Miracles are still the exception; the rule is more nearly that of Rom. 12:1—the daily presenting of ourselves to God as living sacrifices.

This is why I believe the list of the apostles' names in 3:16-19 is not merely a way to end the passage but also itself a statement of the overall paradigm. We are colaborers with Christ, and it is His will to work through the instrumentation of human personality, with all the specificity and uniqueness each of us possesses. Mark didn't simply write down the names so we would have them; he was being used by the Spirit in his writing to show that there is no one-size-fits-all ministry. We do not know a lot about the Twelve, but we know enough to know they were quite different in temperament, outlook, and action. And as we move through the gospel story and the witness of the Early Church, we do not see their respective personhoods being diminished or blended into some kind of "apostolic blob."

Is this a contradiction to my earlier emphasis on the danger of individualism? By no means! It is the biblical distinction between "individuality" and "individualism." The latter is dangerous; the former is of God. And there are some of us in pastoral leadership who need to hear this final point in the deepest parts of our being. Some of us have carried a heavy sense of inadequacy for too long. It may be fueled by life experiences that nearly destroyed our confidence. It may be in being "people pleasers" who hide their true selves in order to gain artificial approval or recognition. It may come from comparing ourselves with others—a leader down the road, or the handful of "religious celebrities" whose ministries seem to be what everyone else should have. It doesn't matter. By whatever road we come to the death "of" ourselves, we have missed the spiritual formation Christ had in mind for the Twelve and the formation He has in mind for us.

Read the list as long as you need to in order to add your name to it. Ponder it until you know that Jesus wants *you* as much as He wanted any of the original apostles.

For some, this will be another expression of courage. We will see in these final verses a call to courageously offer to God ourselves, not "clones" of someone else and surely not a "false" self manufactured for either personal or professional reasons. When Paul spoke to the Ephesian elders for the last time, he told them to keep watch over *themselves*, not merely over the flock in their charge. We must remember that ministry does not flow from a death *of* the self but rather from a death *to* the self. So, we must do whatever it takes to establish and maintain a sense of our uniqueness, our value, and our usefulness to Jesus—and to do it with all the ingredients an authentic and healthy personality requires.[14]

CONCLUSION

And then, in typical Marcan fashion, Jesus and the apostles move immediately into ministry, with the next verse (3:19) saying simply, "then he went home" (NRSV), and in an amazingly brief time, the crowds were again clamoring for His attention to the extent that they could not even find time to eat. What does this tell us? It tells us that "spirituality is reality." All of us can envision a fantasyland spirituality. But that vision is also the virus. To take it in is to destroy the very thing itself.

If you are like me, after you envision the heights and engage your soul in these kinds of commitments and pursuits, the next thing you have to do is "go home"—to your literal house, your particular congregation, your specific community, and so on. Every retreat has an exit as well as an entrance. Wonder quickly becomes work. There is no genuine spiritual formation apart from this realization and this experience. That's why many of our predecessors have used the phrase "ordinary holiness" to describe what all this looks like in the end. Of course we have moments of immense grandeur, but for every one of them, we have a thousand routine experiences. We must give ourselves to the "here" and "now" and refuse to live in the "there" and "later."[15] This means that we will include our primary relationships in our spiritual formation: spouse, children, close friends, and so on. We will honor the age and stage of our lives. We will pay close and continuing attention to those people and things who are near and dear to us.

I take Brother Lawrence as my example for this kind of living. Serving in a monastery kitchen in Paris in the 17th century, he called himself "the lord of pots and pans." His day was virtually consumed with little actions and routine responsibilities. He knew that his spirituality had to be alive and find expression in that context—he had no other. And as he writes in *The Practice of the Presence of God*, he came over time to see that picking up a stick out of the road so a traveler coming later would not trip over it was as much an act of devotion to God as kneeling in the cathedral to receive the holy sacrament.

Years ago, the example of this little man became my picture to emulate. My days are ordinary. My tasks are routine. I have few opportunities to do extraordinary things for God, but a lifetime to do little things for Him. I can be a "stick picker for Jesus." So, where should my spirituality be? It's obvious—in the days of my life as they unfold and as they contain all the particulars attached to them. In fact and in principle, I believe this is the model Jesus began to establish with the Twelve in Mark 3. They would still be working on it at the end of His ministry and at the end of theirs. But if they would do these things, they would glorify God, serve Christ, and find their greatest joy. I believe the same holds true for us today, and so I pass on to you what I am convinced is a pastoral approach to spiritual formation. There's a lot more we could explore, but this much will point us in the right direction.

If you have approached this chapter as I have tried to write it—that is, as an act of devotion to God, then let me invite you to consider concluding it with a time of prayer, using words from the Wesleyan Covenant Service, which I believe express what we have been paying attention to in Mark's account of Jesus' first invitation to the apostles:

> Lord, I am no longer my own, but Yours,
> Put me to what You will.
> Put me to doing. Put me to suffering.
> Let me be employed for You, or laid aside for You,
> Exalted for You, or brought low for You.
> Let me be full, let me be empty.
> Let me have all things, let me have nothing.
> I freely and heartily yield all things
> To Your pleasure and disposal.
> And now glorious and blessed God,
> Father, Son, and Holy Spirit,
> You are mine, and I am Yours. So be it.
> And may the covenant I have made with You on earth,
> Be ratified in Heaven.
> Amen.[16]

Notes

1. I use the term "pastoral leader" in this chapter to describe more forms of ministry than that of local pastor. We are pastoral whenever our ministry calls us to be responsible for others and to be in relationship with them. I am writing with ordained or professional clergy in mind, but I am aware that these same qualities need to be present in lay leadership as well.

2. I will not have time in this chapter to adequately differentiate between "confidence" and "pride," but be sure I am aware of the difference and that I am describing only a healthy, positive sense that arises when our lives are as God wants them to be.

3. Brennan Manning, *The Rabbi's Heartbeat* (Colorado Springs: NavPress, 2003), 97.

4. After more than 20 years of ministry to ministers, I am so convinced of this first point that I am not sure how much progress in our spiritual re-formation is possible

until we develop it in the context of God's amazing love for us. You may want to stay on this point, rather than reading on—until the reality goes to the deepest part of your self.

5. Charles R. Swindoll, *Intimacy with the Almighty* (Dallas: Word, 1996).

6. I know of no better resource to probe this great truth than E. Stanley Jones's *In Christ* (Nashville: Abingdon Press, 1961).

7. Manning, *Rabbi's Heartbeat*, 98.

8. Eugene Peterson has given us a great gift in his book *The Contemplative Pastor*, published in a variety of editions over the years.

9. The Gospel of John reveals Jesus' sense of His one "work" in these passages: 4:34; 5:17-19, 36; 8:26, 28-29; 10:37; 12:49-50; 14:10 and 24.

10. As I write this chapter, much of Christianity is embroiled in defining and debating the phrase "prophetic ministry." Some use it to justify their attempts to overturn scripture and tradition and/or to emphasize an individualistic ministry over against one lived out in community. But that is not what I mean here by being "prophetic." I use the term to mean a courageous determination to represent the faith as given to us in the Bible and in the major creeds of the church. Being "prophetic" as I am using the term does not mean creating a new theology or ethos but rather boldly standing for "the faith once delivered to the saints." And I assure you, both for current society and even much of the church, this kind of "prophetic" ministry is countercultural and requires great courage.

11. If you haven't done so in a while, now would be a great time to go back and read Dietrich Bonhoeffer's classic book *Life Together* (New York: Harper and Row, 1954).

12. John Stott, *Basic Christian Leadership* (Downers Grove, Ill.: InterVarsity Press, 2002), 113.

13. The earliest expressions of monasticism were those of isolated hermits living apart, but over time they came to see that some form of community was necessary. If you'd like to explore this topic further, I recommend John Michael Talbot's book *Hermitage* (New York: Crossroad, 1989).

14. For this reason, I often discover that what pastoral leaders need is not more "religion" (i.e., spiritual discipline or career enhancement), but rather better diet, exercise, sleep and rest, marriage and family life, enjoyable friendships, vacations, counseling, medication, an enjoyable hobby, and so forth.

15. Henri Nouwen was so concerned about an unreal spirituality and a deferred one that he wrote a book titled *Here and Now* (New York: Crossroad, 1994). I recommend it to you.

16. This prayer is found in a variety of sources, including adaptations in wording. See Frank Whaling, ed., *John and Charles Wesley* (New York: Paulist Press, 1981), 387.

William Willimon, S.T.D., is bishop of the United
Methodist Church in Birmingham, Alabama. For 20 years
he was dean of the chapel and professor of Christian
ministry at Duke University in Durham, North Carolina.
He has served as pastor of churches in Georgia and
South Carolina. In 1996, an international survey conducted by Baylor University named him one of the Twelve
Most Effective Preachers in the English-speaking world.
He is the author of 50 books. His articles have appeared
in many publications, including *The Christian Ministry,
Worship,* and *Christianity Today.* His *Pulpit Resource* is used
each week by over 8,000 pastors in the U.S.A., Canada,
and Australia. He serves on the editorial boards of *The
Christian Century, The Christian Ministry, Pulpit Digest, Preaching, The Wittenberg Door,* and *Leadership.* He has given lec-
tures and taught courses at many pastors' schools, colleges, and universities in the United States, Canada,
Europe, and Asia. He is married to Patricia Parker. The
Willimons have two children: William Parker and Harriet
Patricia.

2
The Spiritual Formation of the Pastor:
Call and Community
William Willimon

THE PECULIAR BURDEN OF THE PASTORAL MINISTRY HAS RECENTLY led many to a greater attentiveness to the life of the Spirit. Seminarians, with some notion of what their vocation has gotten them into, ask for courses in spiritual formation. Ministerial spirituality is the "in" subject at pastors' schools. As pastors, we have a duty to lead in the spiritual formation of our people.

But what does it mean for a *pastor* to be formed by the Spirit? My prejudice is that some things take care of themselves, in this case, the spiritual formation of the pastor, as long as we are standing in the right place and looking in the right direction. My goal is to put us in our place.

What does it mean for the Christian called pastor to be formed by the Spirit?

As I read the New Testament, a person gets the Spirit in order to do something with it. The Spirit is there so we might do what God wants done. The Spirit comes upon Mary, a Jewish peasant girl, making her God's singing handmaid. Zechariah, geriatric though he is, is filled with the Holy Spirit so he can prophesy. When the Spirit descends at Jesus' baptism, it is a sign that His ministry has begun.

"The Spirit of the Lord is upon me," Jesus tells them at His homecoming in Nazareth. Why has He got the Spirit? "He has anointed me to preach good news to the poor . . . to proclaim release to the captives and recovering of sight to the blind, to set at liberty those who are oppressed" (Luke 4:18, RSV). As it was for Mary, Zechariah, and Jesus, so it is for us. Hear this early baptismal hymn: "You are a chosen race, a royal priesthood, a holy nation, God's own people, *that you may declare* the wonderful deeds of him who called you out of darkness into his marvelous light" (1 Pet. 2:9, RSV, emphasis added).

In baptism we receive the Spirit in order to be equipped. We are chosen so that we may declare the deeds of God. And of course, the "chosen race" here, the "royal priesthood," *is the baptized*, not simply the ordained.

For Paul, the presence of the Spirit is known by the "fruits of the Spirit," fruits that are ecclesial in nature, the conditions necessary for the church to be the church. The Spirit is ecclesial, functional, activist, and given to enable the church to do God's will. So to be disciplined, formed by the Spirit, is not simply to be, but to do.

Therefore, one cannot talk about the spiritual disciplines of pastors without first asking what, by the Spirit, pastors are for.[1]

What is it that pastors are called by the Spirit to do? Questions about the minister's spiritual life must be secondary to that question. The danger of talking about the minister's spiritual life is that we might take the discipline, formation, and gifts of all Christians and lay these upon a presumed upper class known as clergy. Why should we clergy claim that our vocations require more attentiveness to the Spirit than any other Christian's vocation?

A good way to decide what ministers are for is to examine what the church says and does when it makes a minister. In its rites of ordination, the church designates its clergy.[2] Ordination makes leaders for the church.[3] I have therefore examined the rites of ordination of the Western church. The statement in the old Lutheran ordinal is typical:

> Ministers of Christ are His ambassadors and as such are to preach the Word and administer the Holy Sacraments. They are appointed to wait upon and serve the Church, which is the bride of Jesus Christ, . . . to offer before Him the prayers and supplications of His people; to feed, to instruct, to watch over, and to guide the sheep and the lambs of His flock, whom He hath purchased with His own blood.

Ordination rites indicate that all the baptized share the gifts of the Spirit, the command to evangelize, witness, heal, and serve. But some Christians are designated for the task of equipping the saints, caring for the church, building up the community, and representing the church as a whole. In ordination, the church puts some of its folk under orders; it makes officials "community people."[4]

The essence of the *pastoral* ministry is its "officialness." The pastoral ministry is a function of the church's mission. The pastoral ministry derives its meaning from what needs to occur within the church.

The history of the church contains a long, sad story of how the gifts, graces, and duties that were once part of every Christian's baptismal inheritance were gradually given to the ordained Christians alone. I fear that the current call for a special clerical spirituality could be the latest episode in the ever-present tendency to "clericalize" the church.

In his criticism of the medieval priesthood, Luther said the church is forever acting as if priests are the only Christians who need the Spirit, the only people called to witness, the only royalty of Christ. We must ask Luther's question again in our own day: Are the clergy the only "wounded healers" (Henri Nouwen)? Are pastors the only "sacramental persons" (Urban Holmes)? Are ordained Christians the only "symbol bearers" (John Westerhoff)? No. Ordained persons are a species of a broader genus called "ministry." Any spirituality of the ordained ministry must be derivative of ecclesiology if it is to make sense.

Against medieval definitions of the priesthood, the Reformers asserted that the essence of the clergy is not in some *character indelebilis* conferred at ordination. The only "specialness" of the clergy is its "officialness." The clergy is not an upper crust set over a plebian laity. The essence of the priesthood is essentially relational (whom it serves) and functional (what it does), not ontological (what it is).

The ordained ministry appears to have arisen spontaneously from "below," out of the church and the church's need for leaders. At the same time, rites of ordination claim that it is "from above," a "gift of the Lord" (see Eph. 4:8-11; 1 Tim. 4:14). The ordained ministry is not a status. It is a function. Any polity or theology of ministry, any clerical spirituality that denies this ecclesial base is in error.[5]

I have read few contemporary writers on ministry who say this clearly enough. When people talk about pastors, they cannot resist searching for some peculiar, special attribute that belongs only to pastors and thus legitimates their existence: wounded healer, living reminder, clown, empathetic listener, chief goal-setter, resident dreamer, guru, celibate, prayer expert, male, straight-A seminarian, or other individualistic, natural, or acquired trait that somehow makes a priest "special." This compulsion for specialty implies that the church's need for leadership, service, and edification is not special enough; that the church's authorization needs something else added for it to be holy.

In the ordination rite, hands are laid upon the candidate's head and the church prays an epiclesis, a prayer for the Spirit. This spiritual giftedness is needed to enable the pastor to care for the church. In the words of the prayer for a bishop in the *Apostolic Tradition*, "that thy servant whom thou has chosen as bishop may feed thy holy flock, may exercise thy sovereign priesthood without reproach serving thee day and night . . . and offer to thee the gifts of thy holy Church."[6]

Ask yourself: What is the difference between a pastor who visits, preaches, and baptizes, and any other Christian who does these jobs?

The essential difference is in the *officialness*. My congregation has a dozen laypeople who read Scripture aloud in Sunday worship better than I, and four dozen who visit shut-ins better than I. The difference is that when I do these things, I do them as the "community person," at the authorization of the whole church.

When a pastor visits, teaches, preaches, and baptizes, the church "reads" his or her actions differently from the same actions done by an un-ordained Christian. The pastor bears the burden of our tradition, edifies the body, keeps us together in the church, and represents the whole church.

We pastors are community persons, officials of the church. Any Spirit we have is forming us for this task. Certainly the pastor must walk the journey of faith personally, like any other Christian. But ordination impels the pastor to walk with the whole church in mind. All talk of clergy that neglects the ecclesial origin of the pastoral ministry is dangerous. Permit a historical example: In the Middle Ages, as tension between the church and the world relaxed, monasticism became a kind of second baptism. The monk became the ideal Christian—a special, celibate, totally devoted holy man.

When priestly morality became a problem, Christians talked of the need for the "spiritual formation" of the minister. What was their model for this spirituality? The monk. The way to reform clergy, they reasoned, was to give clergy more features of a *monastic* spirituality. There was talk of a priestly "state of grace"; it was no longer an office but a "state."[7] Ministry became a personal possession, a holy power. A minister became an "altar Christian," a little Christ, a divine mediator through whom grace and wholeness trickled down to the lowly laity. The basis of ministry shifted from a Christological/ecclesial/pneumatological base to a solely Christological one. (This reduction had disastrous consequences in the Vatican's argument against women priests.) Thus spiritual formation is now mainly one-dimensional: the individual soul related individually to God. The basis of the church is primarily Christological—Christ as Lord of this body is the emphasis. Although Christ's ministry is a model for the church's ministry, what I am arguing for in light of all this is a renewed stress upon the ministry. In other words, I am trying to shift the argument about ministry from a debate over who is like Christ (Christology) to a discussion of who best serves Christ's church (ecclesiology).

While we rejoice at the personal, inner "call" of someone into the ministry, historically, such private, inner calls from Christ have more in common with the call to the *monastic* life than to the ancient presbyterate. That is how we get people in seminary who do not want to be pastors. They want to be Christians. The ancient monastic novitiate has thus become seminary. But clergy are not monks. And so Karl Barth says he is suspicious of any effort to cultivate spiritual expertise, *particularly* among the clergy. As far as life in the Spirit goes, Barth wrote shortly before his death, we must all be "beginners," amateurs.

Can you see why I am concerned that two of the most popular writers on ministerial spirituality today are Henri Nouwen and Thomas Merton? We pastors are community persons, not freelance monks. The Spirit calls us to tasks that are ecclesial, relational, and communal, not personal, professional, or universal.

And it is precisely here, in this talk of my being a "community person," that I stop talking about the gifts of the Spirit and begin thinking about the *discipline* of the Spirit.

You see, I'm not a "community person" by natural inclination. Tell me I have some charismatic flair for leadership. Praise me for the art of my preaching or the empathy of my pastoral care, just let me share myself and pour out my feelings, urge me to become a spiritual virtuoso, but please do not yoke me to the Body, do not marry me to that unruly Bride, do not force me to find what I do and therefore who I am among those who gather at my so very mundane congregation.

Let me do freelance ministry, give me a degree and tell me I am special, encourage me to tack up a shingle, allow me to have some exotic spiritual *gnosis* that makes me holy, but do not hold me accountable to the church. I love Jesus, and I want to serve Him. But He married beneath His station. For me the real scandal of ministry, the ultimate stumbling block, the thing I avoid and fear the most, is the church. Like many of you, I set out to serve God and ended up caught among those whom God served. My problem, my difficulty with the Spirit, is that it wants to tie me to the church. The pastoral ministry is so tough,[8] its demands so great, its dependence upon the Spirit essential, because such ministry is a function of the church.

Why have I dwelled so much on the purpose of ministry? Because I am convinced that the spiritual formation of the pastor must be sacramental, corporate, and ecclesial.

Pastors are at the mercy of the Spirit, not for personal gain, but rather to enable them better to serve the church. Prayer, Bible reading, meditation, and devotional exercises are as essential for pastors as for other Christians, but the ultimate goal of ministerial devotional life must be to yoke me more fully to the Body. How? *First, take me back again and again to my call, that authorization that put me where I am and told me what to do.*

I always begin by asking seminarians, how did you get here? Their responses? They tell stories of Sunday School teachers, scoutmasters, and little old ladies and men who first led them toward ministry. The testimony of one young woman was typical: "I read the scripture one Sunday as a lay reader. That was all, just read it. After the service a woman came up to me and said, 'Dear, you read so well. Your reading of that passage did something to me. You should be a minister.'" That is all. But does the call to ministry ever become more holy, more special? In all ordination rites in the

Western church, in the scant but obvious data on the ordained ministry in the New Testament, I hear this simple, mysterious, holy beginning of one person in the church calling another person to the ministry.

But is it enough?

When I was in seminary, James Dittes presented his research on possible psychological reasons for why people go into the ministry. According to Dittes, as children, many pastors were what he calls "little adults." The "little adult" is the child who is the resident adult. The "little adult" is the child who is always the classroom monitor when the teacher leaves the room, the school patrol boy or girl, the child who enforces adult values. The "little adult" may be respected or even admired by other children, but rarely will this child be popular. Dittes' thesis is that "little adults" are attracted to the pastoral ministry. As pastors, they now enforce God's values among wayward adults just as they enforced adult values among wayward children.

One student, upon hearing this, blurted out: "You've just demolished my call into ministry. I thought God called me. You're telling me that my 'call' was little more than my reaction to other people?"

"Has God stopped calling ministers through other people?" asked Dittes.

We are called to leadership in the community of Jesus Christ through the community. The call gets no more blinding and significant than that. Not on a mountaintop or in a cornfield but in the church. And so Calvin speaks of the "twofold" call to the ministry. God calls, but the church must also call. Wesley distinguished the community; any personal, purely individual call is incomplete. As I keep close to God's community, I keep close to my vocation and the necessary spiritual disciplines of my vocation, hearing again the voice that first bid me say yes.

Another spiritual discipline: *I must be renewed by remembering my Lord as my model.* Here I am, seeking a better appointment, a pension, a benevolent bishop, and an all-electric parsonage; and there He is, with a basin and towel, a tray of bread, and a cup of wine red as blood. This is the Christological counterpart of the ecclesiological basis for ministry I have been advocating. He "emptied himself, taking the form of a servant . . . he humbled himself and became obedient unto death, even death on a cross" (Phil. 2:7-8, RSV).

The night an imposing bishop named Tullis laid his hands upon my head and called me a preacher, the Spirit of God got hold of me, not when the choir sang, "Come, Holy Ghost," not in the sermon, not even in the presence of family and friends. It was when the bishop, speaking these ancient words in the service, said: "How great a treasure is committed to your charge. For they unto whom you are to minister are the sheep of Christ, for

whom He gave His life." There I was, wondering, "Will the church sufficiently recognize my superior training and talents? Will I get a washer and
dryer at my next parsonage?" But the words were that the ones who are giv-
en to my care are the ones for whom He *died*.

Thus *the inner discipline of the minister means the discipline of keeping close
to the Body*, close to the ones for whom He died. This discipline takes different forms for different people. For me, this means disciplining myself to
knock on doors and sit down at the kitchen table and visit. I find nothing
about pastoral work more distasteful than visitation—and nothing more essential. Why must it always be me making myself available to them? He
kept close to those He came to save, beside them from His baptism in the
Jordan to the breaking of bread. He had His lonely times apart, His monastic closet of prayer, but in the crush of the crowd, amid the multitude, at tables with them in arguments, beside their beds of pain, in prison, and on
the Cross, He became the model for ministry, pastoral and otherwise.

Finally, a chief spiritual discipline for the pastor is corporate worship. I have
tried to sketch a view of the ordained ministry that is ecclesial, corporate,
and therefore sacramental. Ministerial spirituality must have the same look. I
do not mean to relieve the pastor of the baptismal burden of lifelong spiritual
formation and Wesleyan personal pursuit of holiness. My point is that such
formation must be appropriate to the peculiar nature of pastoral vocation.

Private devotions have their place. But I have chosen to talk not
about private devotions because, for the *community* person, the *pastor*, such
private devotions are but a meager preparation for Sunday, the community
day where our real formation and discipline take place.

Sunday is helpful in keeping my categories clear. I am the deacon, the
server. I wait upon the church by leading its members to God, by pointing
to the Presence in our midst, by feeding and being fed, by preaching the
Word and listening to the Word. Some mornings, to keep things in focus,
amid opening mail, planning meetings, answering the phone, and worrying
about the budget, I practice inner discipline by walking into the sanctuary
and envisioning myself doing those tasks that remind me of who I am. On
Sunday morning in the pulpit, behind the table, at the lectern, handing
people bread, I find myself doing explicitly that which, in other pastoral activities, often remains implicit and inferential. Here is where my vocation
is made visible, ecclesial.

The first stirrings of the ordained ministry in the New Testament are
tied to service at the church's liturgical assembly. Even Paul's apostolate
was *diakonia*, "service," not authority (2 Cor. 1:24; 1 Cor. 3:5; Rom. 11:13;
and other places). The church has leaders—but not as the world conceives
of leadership. "It shall not be so [as it is among worldly leaders] among you"
(Mark 10:43, RSV, and parallels). We are to lead, not by "domineering over

those in your charge," says 1 Peter, but by "being examples to the flock" (5:3, RSV). First Peter also reminds us that it is the *laos*, the "people," who are called to be priests, kings, royalty, and holy (2:9-10). The clergy is called to be servants of the people, not the people called to be servants of the clergy. A sacerdotal clergy desacralizes everybody else. If we can get a "professional" for a minister, why would anyone else in the church want to minister? We clergy never get beyond being deacon.

Why do you think so many of us avoid liturgical functions? Why do we seek some other "specialness"? Why do we demean our preaching, poorly prepare our worship leadership, or trip out on some personal high in personal devotions? Because behind the table and before the Book, who we are becomes visible, explicit, and embarrassingly public. In this scandalous Kingdom, the leaders wait on tables, serve others, wash feet, act foolishly, build others up, and cling to faith, which is social, ecclesial, and corporate.

It gets hard out there. And it would be comforting to believe that there is some spiritual callisthenic, some technique that could help us cope. No. The way to keep going is to remember who chose us, who named us, who ordered us and formed us into this cruciform faith. We may get discouraged, confused by the myriad demands and temptations in the church. So what do we do? We give thanks that ministry need not be self-sustained. Our job is to think about God and God's people, not about the state of our spiritual life. Fortunately, God's self-assigned job is to think about us. We cling to our vocation and are reminded, "You didn't choose Me; I chose you." Thank God it is not a profession; it is a vocation.

In a field education seminar, a young man recounted an episode in a hospital room with an old woman dying with cancer. He had been at the church only two weeks, and confessed, "I was a bit anxious about my first terminal patient."

One morning she said, "Preacher, I want you to pray for me." He tensed up. Prayer. "Well," he thought, "I have not solved all my unanswered questions about prayer. I am not sure."

"What would you like me to pray for?" he asked. (He had had clinical pastoral education at Duke.)

"I'd like you to pray that I'll be healed, of course," she said. "Failing at that, I want you to pray that I won't suffer if I'm not healed."

"Oh no," he thought. "Faith healing. It has come to that. What can I say? How can I keep my integrity?" He hoped a nurse would appear so he could exit.

"But, but I'm just not too sure about what I believe about prayer," he said.

"Not sure, eh?" she said. "Well, we're sure, so you just close your eyes and hold my hand and pray. You'll get the hang of it."

And he, Duke-educated, attractive, smart, closed his eyes and held that lady's frail hand and prayed.

"You know," he said, "she was helped. I could see it. Something happened *in spite of me.*"

And the bishop laid on hands, and the church stood and sang *Veni, Creator Spiritus*, and thereby the church made, and God gave, a new preacher.

I said to that young man, "Someday, at some depressed little church, or worse, some big successful church, you're going to need to remember how you got there, you're going to have to be a pastor even when you don't feel like it, you're going to need to remember who called you and why—someday you'll need to remember. So don't forget that little old lady who helped ordain you."

Do not forget.

Notes

1. In reflecting on the crisis of ministerial identity, H. Richard Neibuhr wrote: "Whenever in Christian history there has been a definite, intelligible conception of the ministry, four things at least were known about the office: what its chief work was and what was the chief purpose of all its functions; what constituted a call to the ministry; and what was the course of the minister's authority; and whom the minister served" (*The Purpose of the Church and Its Ministry* [New York: Harper, 1956], 58). My thoughts in this chapter are organized so that I attempt to speak to each of these conditions.

2. The ordination service for bishop in the Apostolic Tradition of Hippolytus is the basis for later rites. See *The Apostolic Tradition of St. Hippolytus*, ed. Gregory Dix (London: Society for Promoting Christian Knowledge, 1937; reissued by Henry Chadwick, 1968). Examination of this early rite reveals the following: (1) The entire community and its clergy chose the bishop. The person must respond in free will. The local church tests the faith of the bishop to be certain that it is apostolic. (2) Episcopal laying-on-of hands with epiclesis show that, although the community chooses, it is not a purely congregational, autonomous choice. (3) Because the new bishop is chosen by the Body of Christ, the new minister is seen as a gift of the Holy Spirit. Ministry (as Schillebeecher notes) is "from above" (the Spirit) because it is "from below" (the church). In this service we search in vain for any of the alleged attributes of clergy that were ascribed in later years. So little is claimed for ordination. But then, reading on in the document, we note how much is claimed for baptism!

3. A statement by Schillebeecher expresses my conclusions. See *Ministry: Leadership in the Community of Jesus Christ* (New York: Crossroad, 1981), 68.

4. Dr. William Willimon, *Worship as Pastoral Care* (Nashville: Abingdon Press, 1979), chap. 9.

5. My assumptions about ministry imply (as I suppose, do all concepts of ministry) a specific ecclesiology. I see the pastoral, ordained ministry as primarily service (leadership) in the church. One of the sources of present confusion about the nature of the ordained ministry is our inadequate ecclesiology. For instance, the United Meth-

odist *Discipline* states, "Pastors are responsible for ministering to the needs of the whole community as well as to the needs of the people in their charge" (Par. 438.2, *The Book of Discipline*, 1980). Is it accurate to say that ministers are ordained to serve the world at large? If so, what does that say about the ministry of other Christians? Are the distinctions between the church and the world or ordained ministry of other Christian ministry so blurred? It is highly presumptuous for the church to assume that the church's leaders are also to be the world's leaders. The church I have in mind is more exclusive that the extravagantly inclusive statement in the *Discipline* indicates. All Christians are to work with Christ in serving the world at large. Ordained Christians have, as their additional vocation, service to the church in particular.

6. Dix, *Apostolic Tradition*.

7. See Schillebeecher on the writings of Josse Clichtove (1472-1543) in *Ministry*, 58-69.

8. See the essays by Victor Furnish, Paul Achtemeier, and Moody Smith in Earl E. Shelp and Ronald Sunderland, eds. *A Biblical Basis for Ministry* (Philadelphia: Westminster Press, 1981).

Morris A. Weigelt, Ph.D., is professor emeritus of New Testament and spiritual formation at Nazarene Theological Seminary in Kansas City. He received his Th.M. and Ph.D. in New Testament from Princeton Theological Seminary, Princeton, New Jersey. He is well known for teaching, writing, and modeling spiritual formation and the holy life.

3
Living by the Windows of Grace

Morris A. Weigelt

"From his fullness we have all received, grace upon grace"
(John 1:16, NRSV).

"The sure and general rule for all who groan for the salvation of God is this:
whenever opportunity serves, use all the means which he has ordained; for
who knows in which God will meet thee with the grace that bringeth
salvation?" (John Wesley in his sermon "The Means of Grace").

THE CREATOR GOD SEEKS TO GATHER ALL FRAGMENTS OF OUR broken world back together again through His atoning love in Christ. Flora Slosson Wuellner reminds us that God has no garbage cans (John 6:12; Eph. 1:10). He has called pastors to the special role of representing Him— His ambassadors—in that grand reconciling and gathering design and offers them His grace to mold them into vehicles of grace in this shattered and fragmented world. The spiritual formation of the pastor is close to the heart of the Grand Reconciler.

If Dallas Willard is basically correct in his assumption—and I think he is—that the goal of spiritual formation is "an obedience or conformity to Christ that arises out of an inner transformation accomplished through purposive interaction with the grace of God in Christ,"[1] then the strategies by which we identify and access that grace are absolutely critical to the personal spiritual formation of the pastor. The two words that attract our attention in this chapter will be "grace" and "purposive."

To start, I will explore the topic of grace in light of personal spiritual formation. It is all about grace from beginning to end. Healing, molding, and reconciling grace is at the core of the universe.

Next, I plan to investigate some aspects of "purposive." Apart from an intentional strategy, the potential for spiritual transformation is sharply reduced. We are all invited to purposefully position ourselves at the spot where grace shines most vividly in our context. We are all invited into the sunshine and the airy lightness of God's house where the banquet is already prepared—the analogy behind Marjorie Thompson's "soul feast."[2]

My wife and I lived for 29 years in a house featuring beautiful dark wood paneling and only an average number of windows. We have recently moved into a new house featuring light-colored walls and huge windows. Nearly every window, or set of windows, has an arched transom window above it. What a difference the windows make!

In the house of grace it is the size of the windows and our position in front of them that make the difference in the spiritual formation that occurs within. I choose to use the metaphor "windows of grace" to guide this chapter.

REFLECTIONS UPON THE ROLE OF GRACE IN SPIRITUAL FORMATION

It really is all about grace from beginning to end. In a series of lectures at Nazarene Theological Seminary, Thomas Langford of Duke University focused on the nature of grace in the Christian life. Nearly every sentence used the word "grace" one or more times. The very repetition of the word was so powerful that the impact still resonates in my heart and mind. Recently Dr. Langford's students published a book in his honor with the intriguing title *Grace upon Grace: Essays in Honor of Thomas A. Langford.* The title obviously comes from John 1:16, where John writes, "From his fullness we have all received, grace upon grace" (NRSV). *The Message* rewords this verse, "We all live off his generous bounty, gift after gift after gift."

Eugene Peterson paraphrases the words of our Lord in Matt. 11:28-30 in a way that intriguingly captures the role of grace in spiritual formation: "Are you tired? Worn out? Burned out on religion? Come to me. Get away with me and you'll recover your life. I'll show you how to take a real rest. Walk with me and work with me—watch how I do it. Learn the unforced rhythms of grace. I won't lay anything heavy or ill-fitting on you. Keep company with me and you'll learn to live freely and lightly" (TM). The invitation draws all of us directly into the heart of spiritual (trans)formation.

The apostle Paul testified: "But by the grace of God I am what I am, and his grace toward me has not been in vain. On the contrary, I worked harder than any of them—though it was not I, but the grace of God that is with me" (1 Cor. 15:10, NRSV). In a parallel passage in 2 Corinthians he told his detractors and opponents that God had promised him: "My grace is sufficient for you, for power is made perfect in weakness" (2 Cor. 12:9, NRSV). Paul was quick to acknowledge that God's grace was the originating and sustaining strength of his whole life.

The function of grace in saving us and restoring the image of God in our lives is evident throughout Scripture. Paul's words in Eph. 2:8-9 express this truth unmistakably: "For by grace you have been saved through faith, and this is not your own doing; it is the gift of God—not the result of works, so that no one may boast. For we are what he has made us, created in Christ Jesus for good works, which God prepared beforehand to be our way of life" (NRSV). We live a grace-initiated life in Christ. Salvation is a gift only available through grace. Haldor Lillenas was correct when he penned the lyrics "Grace has changed the world I'm living in, / Under the atoning Blood."[3]

Wesley's distinctive emphasis upon sanctifying grace clearly expressed the view that the power of grace is greater than the power of sin, and _entire_ sanctification is a gift of the atoning work of Christ. We are not doomed to a continual struggle against sin—a life of merely settling for sin management. The hymns of the Wesleys express this victory of grace in a variety of wonderful metaphors. The celebration of grace through music is one of the more powerful avenues for growth in Christlikeness.

During 20 years of immersing myself in the literature of spiritual development, I am drawn more and more to the language of formation. Paul uses that language in Gal. 4:19-20: "My little children, for whom I am again in the pain of childbirth until Christ is formed in you, I wish I were present with you now and could change my tone, for I am perplexed about you" (NRSV). The indispensable role of grace in that formation is highlighted throughout Scripture. The apostle John testifies in the opening chapter of his Gospel: "From his fullness we have all received, grace upon grace" (1:16, NRSV).

"Formation," for me, draws a word picture of the variety of forces, events, people, and graces that mold and shape our lives into a Christlike character over a lifetime of devotion to Christ. Formation implies that we are not on a 100-yard dash but on a full marathon. Formation is even visible in the almost unyielding world of rocks—consider the creation of metamorphic rock through the molding of pressure and heat. God is slowly and surely at work in the formation of His representatives and ambassadors—what a gift of grace!

It is instructive to take time in your spiritual journal to reflect upon the range of those graces that shape and form us over a lifetime of devotion. It is helpful to share with a friend the graces that have shaped, molded, influenced, pressured, and heated your personal development in Christ. Give your friend a chance to do the same with you. Both of you will grow in the process.

The followers of Wesley understand theologically that at its most fundamental core, spiritual formation is a product of grace and grace alone. It is deviously easy to confess total dependency upon God as a theological and intellectual concept. It is much more difficult to live it out in daily practice. In the Lord's Prayer we are faced with a daily confession of essential and practical dependency that is, in reality, a regular dress rehearsal for acknowledging and confessing total dependency upon God's grace in much larger and more tragic circumstances—even at the table when we give thanks for the daily bread.

Wesleyans understand quite clearly that there is nothing mechanical or magical about the ways in which the disciplines bring grace into our lives. The disciplines are not ends in themselves, but rather the means by which we strategically position ourselves to allow that grace to do its powerful work in our lives. As Steve Harper wrote: "God does not call us to have a 'devotional time.' God calls us to live a devotional life."[4]

John Wesley himself preferred to call the disciplines "means of grace": "By 'means of grace' I understand outward signs, words, or actions ordained of God, and appointed for this end, to be the ordinary channels whereby he might convey to men, preventing, justifying, or sanctifying grace."[5]

As Wesley investigated the range of the "means of grace," he identified two primary directions from which the grace of God flows into our lives. The first of these is "communion" (with a small "c") that points toward our relationship with God from which grace flows. The second direction is captured by the word "compassion" pointing toward the grace introduced by a relationship with the needy. The devotional life is therefore a combination of communion and compassion—a combination of attention to the inner life of devotion and attention to the outer life of service.

In connection with communion Wesley used the phrase "works of piety," and with compassion he used the phrase "works of mercy." "Works of piety" include the instituted "means of grace" and other actions and duties that directly advance personal holiness—communion with God. "Works of mercy" are the actions that directly foster social holiness—compassion for those who are in need. Both of these sets of "works" reflect the words of Jesus in Matt. 22:37-39: "'You shall love the Lord your God with all your heart, and with all your soul, and with all your mind.' This is the greatest and first commandment. And a second is like it: 'You shall love your neighbor as yourself'" (NRSV).

"Works of piety" as "means of grace" include baptism, prayer, searching the Scriptures, the Lord's Supper, fasting, worship and liturgy, and Christian conference. God chooses to display and convey His grace to His servants through these avenues. Christian conference is an intriguing reference to the wide range of personal relationships that introduce grace to our lives. "Conference" includes family, spiritual friendship, small groups, individual spiritual direction, and ecumenical ties. Wesley not only recommended this "means of grace" but also practiced it regularly and widely. His letters reflect a wide range of "conference" with many different persons.

An interesting self-evaluative exercise is to rank the means of grace in the order of personal usage or in the order of the receipt of grace through their practice. It is often amazing to observe the multifaceted work of God in our lives when we only become more aware of the grace constantly functioning in our environment.

"Works of mercy" as channels of grace fall into three categories in Wesley's discussion. First, he includes "doing no harm" to others. The intent is to watch our actions and words to avoid creating harm for anyone. Second, he includes the obverse, "doing good" to others, with special attention to the poor, the sick, the imprisoned, strangers, and the weak. Wesley quotes the words of our Lord in Matt. 25:31 ff. to show that those who exercise compassion will "inherit the kingdom prepared for you" (v. 34, NRSV), while those who neglect this avenue of grace will be designated as "accursed" and doomed to "the eternal fire prepared for the devil and his angels" (v. 41, NRSV). Third, he writes of "attending upon all the ordinances of God" (NRSV)—evidently directing attention toward the works of piety.

Wesley is keenly aware that all of the means of grace are only avenues to God's grace and have no value in themselves apart from the work of God in our lives. "The sure and general rule for all who groan for the salvation of God is this: whenever opportunity serves, use all the means which he has ordained; for who knows in which God will meet thee with the grace that bringeth salvation?" (from his sermon "The Means of Grace").[6]

Grace provides such a wonderfully dynamic range of gifts that make spiritual life viable and possible—with flair and joy. Lewis Smedes reminds us that "grace is really shorthand for God, who to the amazement of any shamed person, is amazingly gracious. Grace is too unpredictable, too lavish, too delicious for us to stay sober about it. What can you do with such unchecked generosity but smack your lips, slosh it around your tongue, and savor it with joy?"[7]

So the controlling question is, "How do we organize our lives in ways that will allow grace its fullest expression and impact in shaping and forming our lives?"

REFLECTIONS UPON INTENTIONALLY AND PURPOSEFULLY LIVING BY THE WINDOWS OF GRACE

When we intentionally throw open the windows of grace through a strategic and orderly lifestyle, the wind of the Spirit will impact our lives in fresh ways. Wes Tracy long ago observed that the work of the Kingdom is best accomplished by persons still wet and dripping from a fresh touch of the Spirit.

In 20 years of teaching spiritual formation at Nazarene Theological Seminary, one of the most strategic and purposive elements of the course was the introduction of the use of a rule of life to throw open the windows of grace. Following the recommendations of Marjorie Thompson in *Soul*

Feast, we began requiring that the students design a personal rule of life during the course. After consultation and prayer with a small group from within the class, they refined the rule of life. The instructions invited them to practice the rule of life for a period of 90 days. At the end of the 90 days they were instructed to evaluate the success or failure of their personal rule of life with the help of a spiritual accountability friend and then reaim the rule for the next segment of their lives. The final report for the class summarized this whole three-month process.

One of the great privileges of my life has been the reading of these final reports. There is always a sense of being allowed to enter the sacred inner chambers of the heart where the flow of grace has shaped and formed the lives and ministries of my friends. The scars and ravages of sin have profound consequences, but the range and power of grace never ceases to amaze me. My own heart and mind resonate with these reports as I am led to recognize the workings of God's grace in my own life in ways I had never before recognized.

The majority of the spiritual masters across the years have lived by a carefully designed and purposive rule of life. The Benedictines, the Jesuits, and the followers of Ignatius are sterling examples of those committed to a carefully ordered lifestyle structured to maximize the flow of grace into their lives in a corporate setting. Many books have been written about the styles and implications of these examples.

It is equally important for persons to individualize their rule of life. One helpful example is the rule of life Pope John the 23rd designed during his seminary days:

Fifteen minutes of silent prayer upon rising in the morning

Fifteen minutes of spiritual reading

Before bed, a general examination of conscience followed by confession; then identifying issues for the next morning's prayer

Arranging the hours of the day to make this rule possible; setting aside specific time for prayer, study, recreation and sleep

Making a habit of turning the mind to God in prayer.[8]

A rule of life is necessary for appropriate growth. Apart from structure and guidance, the ravages of sin in our lives and the urgent demands of daily living draw us away from attention to spiritual things. Marjorie Thompson uses the garden analogy of the trellis for roses and the stakes for tomatoes to enhance and channel growth. She defines a rule of life as "a pattern of spiritual disciplines that provide structure and direction for growth in holiness. . . . A rule of life, like a trellis, curbs our tendency to wander and supports our frail efforts to grow spiritually."[9] This definition points to the importance of commitment, pattern, structure, and direction in designing a rule of life.

Using the analogy of the windows of grace offers an alternate definition with a more Wesleyan bent:

A rule of life is a personal orderliness [regulation] of daily living that increases the likelihood [possibility, probability] that grace will shape and mold my life into a visible [discernible, noticeable, detectable] Christlikeness in order that I may be a resource of grace to others as I represent Christ in His grand reconciling program.

Designing a rule of life is a fascinating procedure that calls for creative rearrangements of life in order to "learn the unforced rhythms of grace" as we draw upon the "sufficient grace" of God "until Christ is formed" in us. Allow me to make a number of suggestions:

1. Rule: The word "rule" points toward a regulation—an orderliness—of life that is intentional and purposeful. The word "rule" comes from the same Latin word that is the origin of "regulate" and "regulation." The goal is to arrange patterns, structures, and spiritual disciplines into an order that maximizes the probability that grace will break through into life.

One helpful exercise is to reflect upon the ways God has spoken to you most frequently in the past. Becoming sensitive to these avenues of grace will sharpen your focus on the design your rule should take in the present.

A rule is not intended to be restraining, but rather freeing in ways that enhance spiritual growth. The relationship of structure and freedom is critical.

The design should include daily, weekly, monthly, quarterly, and annual rhythms. God chooses to work in multiple rhythms in each of our lives—just as He does in the natural world.

2. Christlikeness: A rule of life without a goal is an imposition upon daily living. Marjorie Thompson chose "growth in holiness" as an objective. The apostle Paul wrote in terms of "Christ-formation." Robert Mulholland in *Invitation to a Journey* suggested that God never blesses us for our own purposes alone, but always shapes and forms our lives that we may serve others. Every time we pray "Thy will be done," we are inviting God to at least give us a bit part in His plan to gather all things together again to himself ("He has made known to us the mystery of his will, according to his good pleasure that he set forth in Christ, as a plan for the fullness of time, to gather up all things in him, things in heaven and things on earth" [Eph. 1:9-10, NRSV]).

Without a goal a rule of life creates resistance and chafing. With a goal the temporary "sacrifices" en route to meeting an all-consuming goal are placed in appropriate perspective. As ministers of the gospel, called to represent God in our world, the call to service through the enabling work of the Holy Spirit frees us to follow our personal rule of life.

The hymn writer was correct when he penned the words "He the great Example is, and Pattern for me."[10]

3. Personal: The word "personal" points to the need to individualize our rule of life in light of our own personality and background and current circumstances. There is no one rule of life that fits all persons.

Some years ago I heard a noted leader in spiritual formation circles give the opinion that 80 percent of the books on how to live a devotional lifestyle have been written by only 20 percent of the personality styles—leaving the majority of us struggling to follow a pattern designed by someone else. The rule of life must be individualized and contextualized.

Reginald Johnson, professor of spiritual formation at Asbury Theological Seminary, offers great insight into this issue in his book *Your Personality and the Spiritual Life*, formerly titled *Celebrate, My Soul*. Using the Myers-Briggs Type Indicator as a guide, he explores the diversity of "soulprint" styles and patterns. "By discovering our own soulprint or personality type, we can appreciate our God-given attributes, identify some of our special areas of vulnerability and weakness, and discover the kinds of resources which might be conducive for nurturing our relationship with Christ."[11]

God chooses to display His grace in wonderfully diverse ways to the widely differing persons He has created. Introverts experience grace in different ways from extroverts. Spontaneous persons will be impacted by grace in ways far different from persons who prefer highly structured life patterns. Persons who specialize in logical analysis access God's grace far different from those who focus on personal interrelationship. Persons who gather data piece by piece recognize God's grace in ways that are different from those who intuitively see the larger picture.

The secret to a successful rule of life is in an individualized design that is attainable for you. Don't set goals so high at first that you become discouraged and drop out of the design.

4. Personal circumstances: A rule of life needs to recognize the circumstances in which you find yourself. Are you a morning person or an evening person? How does your work schedule fit into the design? In what ways do family obligations determine the structure of your life? Physical and emotional limitations call for differing approaches to a life design.

A helpful exercise to identify the issues involved is to take a sheet of paper and divide it into two halves with a line down the middle. On the left, list how you expend your physical, emotional, mental, and spiritual energies. On the right, list how you replace these energies. Upon completion of the exercise, allow the Holy Spirit to guide you to understand more clearly the personal circumstances that impact your rule of life. Allow the Holy Spirit to give you permission to do the necessary reordering suggested in this exercise.

5. Attractions and repulsions: When we begin individualizing our own rule of life, it is attractive to turn primarily to those means of grace most pleasing to our personal preferences. We should always begin with Marjorie Thompson's question: "What am I deeply attracted to, and why?"[12] This question invites us to work through our strengths and preferences to position ourselves to draw upon grace more efficiently and effectively.

It is also valuable to ask the opposite question: "Which of the means of grace are unattractive—even repulsive—to me, and why?" God often chooses to dispense His grace to us through methods that at first appear to us to be weaknesses or, at best, unproductive. Since I had been trained as an analytical scholar, it was difficult for me to believe that God could speak through intuitive channels. Part of my midlife crisis revolved around allowing God's grace to flow into my life from that avenue as well.

The related question is: "Where do I feel God is calling me to stretch and grow at this point in my life's journey?" Each of these questions informs the process of individualizing our rule of life.

6. Personal and corporate: The biblical model of spiritual maturation invites us to incorporate both the personal and the corporate means of grace. The Rule of Benedict often reiterates the search for balance between private and common prayer; between spiritual, mental, and physical elements (I once spent 10 weeks in a Benedictine setting and came to value how work done in community was incorporated into the rhythms of spiritual development) of our being; and between spending time in personal spiritual pursuits and getting involved in the needs of others.

Researching and studying the Lord's Prayer has demonstrated the central importance of the role of community in spiritual formation. A survey of the verbs in the Epistle to the Hebrews startled me into recognizing that God's commands are almost exclusively in the plural. "Far too many modern Christians . . . resist the vulnerability and accountability of community—and they thus bypass one of the required, essential dimensions of spiritual formation and holy living."[13]

7. Accountability: It has been interesting to watch my grandchildren and see how quickly they learn to avoid blame. It is frustrating to watch adults and see how skillful they have become in escaping liability. It is maddening to keep on discovering the ways I sneak out of commitment to my own rule of life.

Committing a rule of life to print is important because it sharpens accountability. It is even more important to have a spiritual friend, spiritual mentor, or spiritual director to help us stay accountable. Periodic reviews of progress or failure in remaining accountable with a spiritual friend or a small group are essential in keeping our rule of life viable.

John Wesley's organization of the early Methodists into societies, classes, bands, and in twin-soul and mentoring relationships was a special gift of grace to the whole church world. Gareth Icenogle argues that "maturity is a product of the daily experience of a small group of people who meet face-to-face with God's face-to-face community in Christ and with one another through the facing power of the Holy Spirit."[14]

8. Discipline and grace: Paul, in 1 Cor. 15:10, articulated the balance between working hard and trusting in grace. There is a delicate balance between carefully and strategically repeating specific patterns in order to position ourselves where grace is most likely to break through and actively resting in God's provisions for spiritual (trans)formation. Please remember that daily rhythms of disciplines may look very different in differing personalities. The old proverb that we should work as if everything depends upon us and trust God as if everything depends on Him contains both a significant truth and a balance we are seeking.

9. Role of service: This is one more reminder that redemptive service to our broken world is part of God's grand reconciling agenda—and a great window of grace. Elizabeth O'Connor's *Journey Inward, Journey Outward* beautifully illustrates this point. "Unless the exercise of the spiritual disciplines eventuates in loving service, they turn out to be—in your case—shallow exercises of halfway discipleship and misguided efforts of self-righteousness. And full self-surrender is the prelude to holy service."[15] The team that wrote *The Upward Call* decided this point was so vital that we dedicated one-fourth of the book to "Finding Ways to Serve Others on Our Journey."[16]

10. Life stages: A rule of life needs ongoing adaptations for the different stages of life. The rule of life for the 30-something minister will look quite different from the rule of life for a 60-something minister. The stretch-points are different, and the trust-points are different. I like the testimony of the older person who had spent a lifetime using music as one of the windows of grace. He testified that now as he sleeps less than he used to, he is invariably awakened to the voice of the Spirit in music. He refers to the process as "hymnsomnia."

11. Specific windows: It would be useful to provide an exhaustive list of the means of grace, but God, as Annie Dillard loves to write, has pizzazz and endless diversity. He is always surprising us with new sources of grace when we seek to be sensitive. The list is actually endless, and the serendipities of grace will never be exhausted. Tidal waves of grace are rushing down the arroyos and gorges of life bringing healing, joy, and reconciliation. Catch the waves!

> "Paint grace-graffiti on the fences;
> Take in your frightened children who
> Are running from the neighborhood bullies
> straight to you" (Ps. 17:7, TM).

12. Hungry and thirsty for God: Bradley P. Holt, in *Thirsty for God;* Marjorie Thompson, in *Soul Feast;* and Ronald Rolheiser, in *The Holy Longing,* use three different root metaphors to remind us that the spiritual formation for which we yearn has been on the heart of God from the beginning. He has been seeking, searching, and longing to rain grace down upon us in a spiritual banquet that will resurrect and revive our thirsty and hungry souls for full-scale participation with the Grand Reconciler in gathering all things to himself.

"Thy Kingdom come
Thy will be done!"

May your rule of life position you before the windows of grace until you become a grace-filled and grace-shaped instrument of grace in God's grand rule of life for the whole universe!

Notes

1. Dallas Willard, *Renovation of the Heart: Putting on the Character of Christ* (Colorado Springs: NavPress, 2002), 22.

2. This is the root analogy Marjorie Thompson uses in her book *Soul Feast* (Louisville, Ky.: Westminster/John Knox Press, 1995).

3. Haldor Lillenas, "Under the Atoning Blood," in *Worship in Song* (Kansas City: Lillenas Publishing Co., 1972), 135.

4. Steve Harper, *Prayer and Devotional Life of United Methodists* (Nashville: Abingdon Press, 1999), 41.

5. *The Works of John Wesley,* 3rd ed. (1872; reprint, Kansas City: Beacon Hill Press of Kansas City, 1979), 5:187-88.

6. Ibid., 200.

7. Lewis Smedes, *Shame and Grace* (San Francisco: HarperSanFrancisco, 1994), 158.

8. Quoted by Marjorie Thompson, *Soul Feast* (Louisville, Ky.: Westminster/John Knox Press, 1995), 139.

9. Ibid., 138.

10. William A. Ogden, "Where He Leads I'll Follow," in *Worship in Song,* 329.

11. Reginald Johnson, *Celebrate, My Soul* (Wheaton, Ill.: Victor Books, 1988), 20.

12. Thompson, *Soul Feast,* 142.

13. Wesley D. Tracy, E. Dee Freeborn, Janine Tartaglia, and Morris A. Weigelt, *The Upward Call* (Kansas City: Beacon Hill Press of Kansas City, 1994), 136.

14. Gareth Icenogle, *Biblical Foundations for Small Group Ministry* (Downers Grove, Ill.: InterVarsity Press, 1994), 281.

15. Tracy, et al., *Upward Call,* 203.

16. Ibid., 201-44.

For Further Reading

Foster, Richard. *Celebration of Discipline*. London: Hodder and Stoughton, 1999.

Holt, Bradley P. *Thirsty for God*. Minneapolis: Augsburg Fortress, 1993.

Norris, Kathleen. *Amazing Grace: A Vocabulary of Faith*. New York: Riverhead Books, 1999.

Thompson, Marjorie. *Soul Feast*. Louisville, Ky.: Westminster/John Knox Press, 1995.

Tracy, Wesley D., E. Dee Freeborn, Janine Tartaglia, and Morris A. Weigelt. *The Upward Call: Spiritual Formation and the Holy Life*. Kansas City: Beacon Hill Press of Kansas City, 1994.

Weavings: A Journal of the Christian Life. Published by Upper Room Ministries® (www.weavings.org).

Weigelt, Morris A. and E. Dee Freeborn. *Living the Lord's Prayer: The Heart of Spiritual Formation*. Kansas City: Beacon Hill Press of Kansas City, 2001.

Willard, Dallas. *The Divine Conspiracy: Rediscovering Our Hidden Life in God*. San Francisco: HarperSanFrancisco, 1998.

———. *Renovation of the Heart: Putting on the Character of Christ*. Colorado Springs: NavPress, 2002.

E. Dee Freeborn, A.B., B.D., D.Min., is professor emeritus of spiritual formation at Nazarene Theological Seminary in Kansas City, where he also served as director of the chapel. He received his D.Min. in spiritual formation from Asbury Theological Seminary. He is author of the book *When You Pray,* a contributing author to *The Upward Call,* and coauthor with Dr. Morris Weigelt of *Living the Lord's Prayer.* He also teaches spiritual formation in local churches and in a variety of retreat and conference settings.

4
Foundations for a Life of Prayer

E. Dee Freeborn

❧ IN RECENT DAYS A SEEMINGLY SIMPLE QUESTION CAPTURED MY attention. "What are the elements necessary for a life of prayer?" In other words, what's the bottom line to an effective prayer journey with God? The question assumes a saving relationship with the Lord Jesus Christ. But beyond that, what is it that cannot be left out if a person is serious about developing a prayerful communication with God? Maybe the question is not so simple after all!

I'm sure I don't have all the answers, but let me share some of the ideas that have been dawning on me.[1] You can improve on these concepts I'm sure, but let's at least think together on this vital issue.

INTENTIONALITY

A crucial foundation to a worthwhile prayer life is *intentionality*. Without intention, prayer will not happen, except in the moments of life's emergencies. We are all acquainted with "foxhole" prayers of one kind or another.

I'll never forget the morning I was driving to work in three lanes of rush-hour traffic. A Midwest spring rainstorm was making it difficult for all of us to see. Up ahead, I happened to see all the taillights go on and instinctively I hit the brakes. My little Honda Accord hydroplaned and went into a 360-degree spin. Being in the middle lane, I swerved across a lane of traffic, spun into the median ditch, and came to rest facing the right direction, all without a scratch!

I remember my prayer so well. It went something like, "Oh God, oh God, oh God!" Not very elegant, but at least my thoughts were in the right direction.

When life comes crashing in, the human spirit instinctively calls to the Creator. But that is not the kind of praying we are giving attention to here. A life of prayer happens only when we *intend* to pray.

47

The prayer life of Jesus is always instructive. In Mark 1:35 we read, "Very early in the morning, while it was still dark, Jesus got up, left the house and went off to a solitary place, where he prayed." No happenstance praying here. You can feel the purposeful, deliberate choice He has made to pray.

The trouble with *intentionality* is that it sounds so much like *commitment* or *discipline*, and we don't like those words. We don't want them to apply to the life lived in the "freedom of the Spirit," but they do! If I am going to nurture a mature life of prayer, then I will *intend* to do it. I will make the commitment necessary! If I do not begin here, then I should not be too surprised if I end up with an impotent prayer life.

It's interesting—I have no trouble with this concept when it comes to anything else worthwhile in life. If I dream of becoming an artist, musician, teacher, minister, mechanic, or whatever—without intentionality, without commitment, it will never happen.

Why then is intentionality in prayer such a problem? If we assume that prayer is conversation with God, then to be an intentional conversationalist is to make the commitment to listen. Fruitful and meaningful conversation is never one-way.

But my commitment and determination to listen also has its obstacles. It will involve loss of control. I am now willing to move from the center and allow God to speak. It also involves risk. What if what I hear is more than I bargained for?

My heart's longing may be for a vibrant prayer relationship with the Heavenly Father, but without intention it will never happen.

One of the most vivid illustrations of intention occurred in our own home. Our son, Dan, wanted to learn Tae Kwon Do karate at the age of five. The instructor believed he was too young and told him to come back when he was six. On his sixth birthday he asked again if he could take lessons. He became a black belt at the age of nine. Without intention, it would have never happened.

As you think about this foundation of intentionality, how would you finish this sentence? "If I were to permit someone to look over my shoulder at the intentionality of my prayer life, it would be easy to conclude . . ."

Consistency

A second vital foundation to an ongoing prayer life is *consistency*. I am not suggesting here a regulated timetable that others ought to follow. The issue is pattern. When viewed over a given length of time, is prayer evident in any consistent manner in my life? The design may have holes and gaps here and there, but does a visible pattern appear?

Again, Jesus sets the paradigm. Not only did He pray early in the morning, but He also prayed at other times as well. "After leaving them, he went up on a mountainside to pray. When evening came, the boat was in the middle of the lake, and he was alone on land" (Mark 6:46-47). "One of those days Jesus went out to a mountainside to pray, and spent the night praying to God" (Luke 6:12). "But Jesus often withdrew to lonely places and prayed" (5:16).

Prayer was such a consistent occurrence in His life that it was evident to anyone who knew Him at all. His life of prayer invited the disciples to ask Him to teach them how to pray. His intentionality and consistency were compelling! There was a rhythm of prayer to His life and ministry. It was into the crowds to heal and restore, then getting alone to pray, then back to ministry with the multitudes, and withdrawing again to be with the Father.

Whereas intentionality speaks of commitment, consistency points to obedience. Intentionality is only "good intentions" without the follow-through of consistent obedience. Do I respond to Jesus' call to prayer with any pattern at all?

Those who study the development of values and how we develop our value systems indicate that one of the definitions of a value has to do with pattern. If something is of value to us, it will appear as part of the composition of our lives. To proclaim, for example, that we value prayer but not have it show up with any consistency in our daily living might mean that prayer is a goal or desire or a strong wish but not a value as yet. I may "value" Bible reading, but unless there is some kind of pattern of Bible reading in my life, I probably should call it something else, but not a value.

Again, it was our son's study of karate that illustrated so vividly the importance of consistency, of pattern. While in elementary school, his friends would call after school. If we said he was not home, their first response would be, "Oh, is he at karate?" The pattern was obvious, and for Dan, it was a value.

For several years I was privileged to serve as an associate pastor with the late Dr. Earl G. Lee, pastor emeritus of Pasadena First Church of the Nazarene. No one needed to guess about his life of prayer. It was obvious, and the pattern was clear for all to see. In the mornings he could be found in his home office in prayer and sermon preparation. He began the Friday morning Early Christians prayer meeting, a place of spiritual energy for those headed off to work. Prayer permeated his ministry.

I have come to realize that those who seem to pray so effortlessly and constantly have built their prayer sojourns by intention and consistency. They made a commitment and were obedient. What I am privileged to witness is the overflow!

Take some time to reflect on how you pray, and then consider how you would finish this sentence. "As I look at the pattern of consistency in my prayer life, I see . . ."

EXPECTANCY

We have proposed that where intentionality spoke of commitment, consistency suggested obedience and discipline. It is not surprising that anything worthwhile in life begins with these two building blocks. It is no less true in growing a life characterized by a pattern of prayer.

A third foundation to effective prayer is *expectancy*. Praying is not just another duty or obligation in the list of Christian "oughts." We do not pray in order to qualify as a good Christian. Rather, we come to the Father with expectancy. When our children came to us with their Christmas hopes and dreams, you can put it down that they were also expecting something!

Expectation speaks of faith and of hope. What then should I *expect* (have faith for) when I pray?

First, I can expect a *presence*. I have faith that when I come to the secret place of prayer, my Heavenly Father will be there to meet me. He *wants* to be with me; He wants me to know Him. The whole of John 17, Jesus' high-priestly prayer, demonstrates an acute awareness of the presence of the Heavenly Father. There is no empty, dutiful praying here; there is communication and communion!

Second, I can expect a *hearing*. Part of the drawing and attraction to prayer is the belief that I *will* be heard! It is the living, personal, hearing God who waits for me to come into His presence. Isaiah declares, "O people of Zion, who live in Jerusalem, you will weep no more. How gracious he will be when you cry for help! As soon as he hears, he will answer you" (30:19). The psalmist assures us, "The LORD will hear when I call to him" (4:3). As John boldly declares, "This is the confidence we have in approaching God: that if we ask anything according to his will, he hears us. And if we know that he hears us—whatever we ask—we know that we have what we asked of him" (1 John 5:14-15).

And finally, I can expect a God who *answers*. "Call to me and I will answer you and tell you great and unsearchable things you do not know" (Jer. 33:3). Jesus promises, "So I say to you: Ask and it will be given to you; seek and you will find; knock and the door will be opened to you" (Luke 11:9). Jesus even goes on to proclaim, "If you remain in me and my words remain in you, ask whatever you wish, and it will be given you" (John 15:7).

Oswald Chambers puts the case succinctly and his comments are worth quoting in full:

> Jesus never mentioned unanswered prayer, He had the boundless certainty that prayer is always answered. Have we by the Spirit the unspeakable certainty that Jesus had about prayer, or do we think of the

times when God does not seem to have answered prayer? "Every one that asketh receiveth." We say—"But . . . , but . . ." God answers prayer in the best way, not sometimes, but every time, although the immediate manifestation of the answer in the domain in which we want it may not always follow. Do we expect God to answer prayer?[2]

In other words, with the faithful children of God, it is "faithed" or "believed" that God will answer, be it many times in a way we had not anticipated. The calm assurance of asking prayer was vividly displayed to us when our daughter, Dana, was in elementary school. She was diagnosed with an ear problem that called for surgery. On the morning of the operation my wife called Pastor Earl Lee and asked if he could come and pray and anoint Dana before we left for the hospital.

We gathered around the living-room coffee table, knelt, anointed Dana, and prayed for her. It was simple, quiet, no parades, no fanfare, just faith that this was the thing to do.

At the doctor's office for a checkup before going to surgery, the physician came back and said, "I don't know what has happened, but this girl does not need surgery," and proceeded to cancel the operating room.

Expectancy or *prayer in faith* is not the same as *faith in prayer*. Maxie Dunnam puts it this way:

> Certainly *faith in prayer* may be presumptuous and clamorous, presenting ultimatums to God and demanding his acquiescence. But *prayer in faith* is different. It may ask and keep on asking. Indeed it may be clamorous. But all that the asking and pleading is, is entire submission to the will of God. Our faith is not in prayer, but in God. In prayer we may plead passionately for our need, but our faith is in God; thus we can close our petitions as Jesus did, "Thy will be done."[3]

HUMILITY

This brings me to the fourth essential foundation in a life of prayer, that of *humility*. Humility speaks of submission and of rest. As Dunnam has suggested, if my faith is in prayer (which usually means obvious, positive answers), then I may be in trouble. However, to pray in faith (or expectancy) is to be willing to acknowledge the sovereignty of God and His right to answer my prayer in any way He deems best for me. In fact, that is exactly where my faith resides, that in all things God is working for the good of those who love Him (Rom. 8:28).

Humility is to realize that there is no higher prayer (and probably none more difficult) than "Thy will be done."

It is significant to me that at the end of His ministry, Jesus, the Son of God, ended His prayer in Gethsemane with such a declaration (Matt. 26:42). He prayed with deep earnestness and anguish but did not get what

He asked for. He therefore relinquished His will to that of the Father and aligned himself with the Father's will. The answer to prayer here seems to me to be alignment, not deliverance.

To pray with humility is a stance before God. It is the approach, the way I enter in His presence. I may come with heartfelt requests, honest petitions, but always with humble respect for the sovereign God of the universe, the One who answers as He wills.

We need to acknowledge that praying "Thy will be done" can be approached in at least two ways. One is to see it as fatalistic and hopeless. It is to decide that the situation is so far gone that I end up praying in a spirit of resignation. Or somehow we see the formula "Thy will be done" as absolutely essential to the answer, an obsession with method or ritual rather than a focus on the loving Father. This can lead to despair, discouragement, and depression when the answers are not what we planned on hearing.

The other approach is to pray out of faith and deep trust in the One who died and lives again! This is the God who paid the ultimate price for our redemption and who loves us beyond our comprehension. He *wills* the very best for us and sees to it that His will is carried out! I can pray in true submission and rest, "Nevertheless, Thy will be done"!

What an honor it is to address the holy God, to come into His presence with boldness. To think that He would stoop to listen and hear me, that is good enough. How and when He answers matters little in the light of His willingness to shower me with His grace and live His life through me. What more could I ask?

As we think about this foundation of humility, a reflection for personal discovery might be: "If I were to pray the Gethsemane prayer, 'Not my will, but thine be done,' my prayerful approach to complex problems would . . . ."

SERENITY

It is difficult to think about foundations to an effective life of prayer without mentioning silence and solitude. Silence and solitude have been an integral part of Hebrew and Christian spirituality. To me, one of the most stunning passages in the Old Testament is found in Eccles. 5:1-3:

> Guard your steps when you go to the house of God. Go near to listen rather than to offer the sacrifice of fools, who do not know that they do wrong. Do not be quick with your mouth, do not be hasty in your heart to utter anything before God. God is in heaven and you are on earth, so let your words be few. As a dream comes when there are many cares, so the speech of a fool when there are many words.

I have often wondered what might happen if, over time, we were to read this passage every Sunday morning before entering the worship service?

Silence

Have you ever "felt" the silence? It can happen in those serendipitous moments when all the clatter and clanging around us suddenly ceases and you almost "feel" the silence. For some, such silence is a comfort to the soul, a healing for a shattered spirit, and a source of deep *serenity*. For others, such absence of noise becomes threatening and even terror-filled.

Ours is a noisy world. Even as I write, the noises find their way into my office sanctuary. A vacuum is roaring away as it devours the dirt and grime of a hallway carpet. Traffic hums and swooshes its frantic way past my window. Trains fill the air with their mournful railroad-crossing whistles. Wherever I go in my world, there is noise—radio, television, traffic, and people.

No wonder our hearts are noisy too. How can they be otherwise? The younger generation appears to be "wired for sound." Whether walking, skateboarding, driving, or studying, they are not far from noise. Most of the time they are immersed in it. Sound engulfs their minds and souls through earphones that are barely visible.

While the young may have their challenges with technology and music, as a minister, I find that I live in a world made noisy by words. I deal so much with words that they can clutter my mind and heart with their noise. Not only so, but also the words themselves can become empty, drained of their meaning. Henri Nouwen, speaking about us ministerial types, reminds us: "When our words are no longer a reflection of the divine Word in and through whom the world has been created and redeemed, they lose their grounding and become as seductive and misleading as the words used to sell Geritol."[4] (You can substitute about any product name for Geritol.)

How God comes to us in silence is accented in the fascinating story of Elijah found in 1 Kings 19:9-12. Elijah waits for God outside his mountain retreat. Three astounding events occur. First, Elijah encounters a rock-splitting wind, then comes a ground-shattering earthquake, and finally an earth-scorching fire. Surely God would appear in at least one of those cataclysmic happenings. What a dramatic and "Godlike" entrance that would be! But instead, the Lord of heaven is discovered in—a whisper. A whisper! A still, small voice.

When we are encouraged by Scripture to "be still, and know that I am God" (Ps. 46:10), we ought to pay attention. Stillness can bring serenity in our shattered, chaotic world. To be still is not all that easy, but it *is* possible. Even Jesus found it necessary to get away from those around Him and be alone. In the quiet He found the serenity that brought strength in a poured-out ministry.

We know that silence can mean "the absence of noise," but it is also instructive to know that there are differences between one noise and another. Researchers say that there is a difference between the decibels of sound generated by heavy city traffic, for example, and the same level of decibels created by a waterfall. My neighbor's rackety lawn mower impacts my spirit in a way different from the morning chorus of chickadees and cardinals in the trees nearby. If it's morning, I awake in a different mood to that lawn mower's growling than I do to my feathered friends singing!

We need to consider not only the sounds that are healthy and creative but also the possibility that our hearts and our ministerial lifestyles need periods of worshipful silence. I say worshipful, for some silences are deadly. The growing silence between estranged marriage partners and the sudden silence of a teen contemplating suicide are deadly silences.

I can be silent enough to hear God "in a whisper." When I ask myself certain questions, I begin to discover where the possibilities are for more quietness in my life. For example, in my daily schedule, where is that one time or place that provides the opportunity for silence? In the recent past, that time for me has been just after rising in the morning, before anyone else in the family is awake. With no reading or radio or activity of any kind, I sit and "soak up the silence." It gives my noisy heart a chance to begin the day quietly—with God.

Are there any "islands" of silence in my day that I might be overlooking? How's my progress in weaning myself away from the incessant noises of television, radio, and the CD player? As I ask these questions and others, I'm made aware and encouraged that there are some ways to deal with my noisy heart after all.

When noise and words dominate my life, then my prayers can drift into nothing more than performances for God. Henri Nouwen says it best in *The Living Reminder:* "Thinking about my own prayer, I realize how easily I make it into a little seminar with God . . . thinking profound thoughts and saying impressive words. I am obviously still worried about the grade!"[5] It is when I am learning how to be quiet and "still" that I begin to discover the depths and riches of "knowing God."

Solitude

Solitude is easier for some than it is for others, but the Scriptures indicate that this practice is important for all of us. While instructing His disciples in Matt. 6:5-8, Jesus said, "When you pray, go into your room, close the door and pray to your Father, who is unseen" (v. 6). During His powerful public ministry, He also practiced solitude at crucial moments. Surely they contributed to His sense of serenity and stability in life's situations.

In preparation for His life's mission, He spent 40 days alone in the desert (Matt. 4:1-11). When needing wisdom in choosing the Twelve, He spent the night alone (Luke 6:12). He chose a lonely mountain for the

Transfiguration (Matt. 17:1-2). It was a long and lonely night in the Garden of Gethsemane (26:36-44). After feeding 5,000, He went to a mountain to be by himself (14:23). In Luke 5:16, He withdrew to lonely places. After a long night of work, He rose early and went to a solitary place (Mark 1:35).

What a dissonant topic for ministers like us. We are so busy. There is so much to do that seldom do we find periods in which we do not know what needs to be done next. We are so swept along by the "musts" and "oughts" of life that there is no time to wonder if all that we do is _worth_ doing.

Why is solitude so important? First, it is the place where we meet our Lord, to be with Him. The reason for being alone is found in 1 John 1:1: "That which was from the beginning, which we have heard, which we have seen with our eyes, which we have looked at and our hands have touched —this we proclaim concerning the Word of life." If I want that level of fellowship with my Lord, I will have to be responsible for creating moments of solitude. My culture certainly will not give it to me!

Second, in solitude I find that prayer is not valuable because "it works" but because there is a value in prayer itself. To commune with the risen Christ, to be _with_ Him, is far more valuable than all the "results" of prayer, as blessed as they may be.

Third, it is in solitude that I begin to evaluate my world with more clarity and discernment. This materialistic culture tries its best to convince me that what I own is how much I'm worth, and who I am is to be evaluated on the basis of what I do. Henri Nouwen puts it so clearly: "It is in this solitude that we discover that being is more important than having, and that we are worth more than the result of our effort."[6]

There is a subtle trap here. To be alone with God is not all there is to the transforming Christian journey; it is only a part of it. In reality, those who find time to be alone with the Lord find heightened sensitivities to the suffering, the poor, and the marginal among us. Nouwen reminds us, "In and through solitude we do not move away from people. On the contrary, we move closer to them through compassionate ministry."[7]

What are some ways into solitude, in the midst of our jam-packed schedules and frenetic lives? A beginning is to find that place of quiet that is right for you. Where in your home is an area that can be made into your "solitary place"? What about the "moments of solitude" that dot our days? They occur throughout the day if I will but look for them. Have you considered personal retreats, monthly, yearly? They may be hours or days out of the city or in a quiet corner of the public library. The options are many.

Solitude helps put our world into perspective. I've often wondered why the Church does not seem to make more of a difference in the world. Maybe our impotence in changing the world is due, in part, to our addiction to the world. Solitude with the living Lord can help break that addiction.

Notes

1. These concepts first appeared in my book *When You Pray*. They have been revised, updated, and used by permission.

2. Oswald Chambers, *My Utmost for His Highest* (New York: Dodd, Mead, and Co., 1935), 147.

3. Maxie Dunnam, *The Workbook of Intercessory Prayer* (Nashville: Upper Room, 1979), 25.

4. Henri Nouwen, *The Way of the Heart* (New York: Seabury Press, 1981), 47-48.

5. Henri Nouwen, *The Living Reminder* (New York: Seabury Press, 1977), 52.

6. Bob Benson, *Disciplines for the Inner Life* (Waco, Tex.: Word Books, 1985), 35.

7. Nouwen, *Way of the Heart,* 22.

For Further Reading

Balthasar, Hans Urs von. *Prayer*. San Francisco: Ignatius Press, 1986.

Bloom, Anthony. *Beginning to Pray*. New York: Paulist Press, 1970.

Foster, Richard. *Prayer: Finding the Heart's True Home*. San Francisco: Harper, 1992.

Hunter, Bingham. *The God Who Hears*. Downer's Grove, Ill.: InterVarsity Press, 1986.

Hybels, Bill. *Too Busy Not to Pray*. Downer's Grove, Ill.: InterVarsity Press, 1988.

Lochman, Jan. *The Lord's Prayer*. Grand Rapids: Eerdmans, 1990.

Nouwen, Henri. *The Way of the Heart*. New York: Seabury Press, 1981.

———. *The Living Reminder*. New York: Seabury Press, 1977.

Oates, Wayne. *Nurturing Silence in a Noisy Heart*. Garden City, N.Y.: Doubleday, 1979.

Reginald Johnson, Ph.D., has been a member of the faculty at the Wilmore, Kentucky, Campus of Asbury Theological Seminary since 1978. He is the past chair of the Area of Preaching and Worship and has also served as director of Supervised Ministry and director of the Doctor of Ministry Program. Dr. Johnson received his Ph.D. from Edinburgh University, Scotland, and is an ordained elder in the North Carolina Conference of the United Methodist Church, where he served as pastor for several years before going to Asbury. He is involved in the ministry of spiritual direction, speaks frequently at conferences, leads retreats, and teaches continuing education courses and workshops in the area of spiritual life and prayer. He is the author of *Celebrate, My Soul,* which has been rereleased under the title of *Your Personality and the Spiritual Life.* His two-CD multimedia short course on prayer, *Learning to Pray Again,* is available through Cokesbury. He has also written numerous articles on various aspects of the Christian life. Dr. Johnson is certified by the Association for the Application of Psychological Type and is an approved evangelist and Bible teacher for the United Christian Ashram Movement. He has served on the Jessamine County School Board and as a coach in Little League and Babe Ruth Baseball. Dr. Johnson and his wife, Diane ("Jo"), have four children: Wesley, Joshua, Katie, and Nathan.

5
Ways We Pray:
Deepening Intimacy by Spending Time with God
Reginald Johnson

🔥 THE LIGHT BLUE '48 DODGE WOUND ITS WAY UP THE MOUNTAIN until it finally rounded a bend in the dirt road, disappearing behind a clump of mountain laurels. Realizing that my heart was in my throat, my newly assigned camp counselor tried to loan me a little of his strength by giving my hand a comforting squeeze. I was already so homesick that I could hardly breathe. It was my first time away from home. How could I possibly live an entire week without my parents?

We were kept busy the rest of the day, and I was so weary when bedtime finally came that I drifted off to sleep in my strange new surroundings. It was about two o'clock in the morning when something awakened me. I thought someone had touched my shoulder. I opened my eyes and looked around the rustic cabin. I could see my other buddies sleeping in their bunks, and across the way was my counselor, fast asleep. But the room seemed filled with a warm, loving presence. Although I couldn't see Him, God seemed so near that I could have reached out and touched Him. I knew with the instincts of a child that *He* had awakened me. He was assuring me that He was with me and that everything would be OK. I talked to Him silently for a few minutes before I drifted off, falling asleep in His presence in the early morning darkness.

It is my earliest memory of praying. And now, whenever I start complicating the simplicity of prayer, God seems to use that memory to recall me to the basics:

- Prayer doesn't originate with us, but God seeks us out, "speaking" in whispered intimations and "knocking" with gentle nudges, in order to evoke a response or encourage an invitation from our side.
- God loves us and wants to spend time with us.

- God is personal, relates to us in personal ways, and has given us the gift of prayer so that we can be with Him and deepen our friendship with Him.
- Prayer is not so much something that we have to do, one more thing to add to the long list of our tasks and obligations to fulfill; but it is a way of being in a loving, trusting relationship with the living Christ. It is a way of "doing life" with God.

DEEPENING FRIENDSHIP

Prayer is God's gift for deepening our relationship with Him. We can perceive the implications of this by reflecting on our friendships. Consider how closeness develops. Two things are essential. First, we must be willing to give of ourselves to the other person. In other words, we must be ready to be self-disclosing, sharing our thoughts and feelings in honest ways. Otherwise, how would the other person ever sense that he or she really knew us?

However, if our relationships were only characterized by our being in control of the conversation, constantly giving our thoughts and feelings to the other person, those relationships would become very shallow and short-lived. To grow, a second thing is required. Besides being willing to share ourselves, we need to be open to others, allowing them to be self-sharing with us.

Those two aspects of personal relationships in the human realm have corollaries in our friendship with God. Deepening friendship with God also requires giving *and* receiving. Prayer in the giving mode is active—pouring out our hearts or expressing our highest thoughts to God. But there is also a receptive side in a growing companionship with God—becoming quiet, attentive, listening, noticing God's activity, realizing experiences of God's presence, appreciating God's gifts, and enjoying God's goodness.

Another thing about human relationships with implications for our style of relating to God is that there are myriad ways we can be with one another that deepen our relationship. Sometimes we are sharing our hearts; at other times we are working side by side on some mutually important project. Sometimes we are joining together in a pleasurable activity; at other times we are sitting quietly at a friend's side. There are all kinds of ways of being with one another that draw us closer and more deeply together. In the same way, when it comes to prayer, there are a multitude of ways we become conscious of God's presence with us, and countless ways we may spend time with Him, sharing our lives with Him and allowing Him to share His own life with us.[1]

PRAYING WITH OUR SENSES

God apparently delights in capturing our attention by such things as a flock of Canadian geese flying in formation on a quiet fall evening, endless waves washing over sandy beaches, daffodils, starry nights, sunsets, mountain vistas, puppies, waterfalls, and playful children. What is needed from our side is a willingness to "waste time" appreciating, relishing what is right in front of our noses. Such experiences evoke a host of feelings—wonder, awe, reverence, and gratitude. Prayer arises as we treasure these moments as gifts from the Father's hand, responding spontaneously to Him in the ways that are most natural for us. We may invite God to be with us as we listen to soul-inspiring music, paint a picture, play our favorite piece on a guitar, take a jog, or work in our garden. Such activities become prayer as we do them in God's presence. We realize that the joy and satisfaction they bring are actually blessings He is giving. We may sit in our favorite chair holding a well-worn Bible in our lap, with a lit candle or a few cut flowers in a little vase on the table next to us, and a cross or a collage of pictures of our loved ones hanging on the wall before us, and these familiar and special things help make us aware we are in God's presence. The space we have created reminds us we are on holy ground. We can pray with our senses.

PRAYING WITH OUR IMAGINATIONS

Scripture abounds with stories, parables, metaphors, and analogies. As we read such material, we can allow ourselves to be drawn into the images depicted. Word pictures can trigger our imaginations. We can mentally re-create scenes and identify with the characters. We can relate to the feelings expressed in a psalm, allowing them to remind us of similar feelings in our own lives and the situations that prompted them. We may dwell on some metaphor, turning it over again and again, moving down from the surface to meanings and associations that connect with our lives. As we do, God is involving us in a kind of "dialogue" with himself.

We can pray over our dreams, talking to God about the feelings with which they leave us, reflecting on the symbols they contain, and bringing to Him the situations in our daily life to which they point. Imaginative prayer can also be inspired by objects that point beyond themselves to some larger reality—a letter that, because of its timeliness, may symbolize God's providential care; a special pebble that may remind us of the goodness of a grandparent from whose grave it came; a ring that will always stand for the love with which a spouse has filled our lives.

Our daydreaming can lead us into God's presence as we follow the flow of ideas and images that bubble to the surface of our minds when we are relaxed and receptive. They may speak to us of noble aspirations or of unholy dispositions; we may become aware of inspired ideas or of dark fantasies. Any and every thing can be turned into prayer. We can pray with our imaginations.

Praying with Our Minds

We can spend time with God as we reflect and think deeply about things. We may mull over a life experience, remembering the details, objectifying what happened and our reactions to the event. As we perceive things as they are and consider what our reactions say about ourselves as persons who respond in such a manner, this honest reflection can become a prayer of self-examination. God is on the side of reality.

We may call upon this capacity to analyze, sift, sort, and compare as we read a passage from the Scripture, soaking in the meaning of the words, meditating on them, distilling the truth they present about God or ourselves. When we enter into the meaning of the text, connecting and applying it to the various situations of our lives, we are giving God a chance to speak to us through His Word. He uses the process to reframe the way we look at life situations and refashion our patterns of responding to the circumstances. Our lives are being "shaped by the word."[2]

We may read from a theological book that turns our thoughts to understanding what God is like and recognizing what God is doing, and that stimulates reflection about living in correspondence to this truth we are discovering by our decisions, resolutions, and actions.

We may engage in polemical prayer as we wrestle with God over some challenging scripture or argue with God over some difficult life situation. Confrontational prayer may pour from our thoughts as we respond to God who is challenging us to integrity, responsibility, or justice; or as we give voice to our complaints, anger, troubles, and struggles.[3] We can pray with our minds.

Praying with Our Hearts

We deepen our relationship with God when we talk to Him conversationally, taking the time to express our feelings about things that really matter to us. We talk to Him about our feelings, not because He is unaware of them, but because such self-sharing deepens friendship. Our feelings give us the capacity for empathy. We can identify with others and talk with the Lord about what they are going through. We can open ourselves to the yearnings that God has for others so that our words are joined to His will and are expressions of His heart's desire. Prayer as recollection may lead us into memories, rehearsing experiences, awakening gratitude and praise. Sometimes words just get in the way. We will simply rest in God's presence, allowing Him to quiet our souls and refresh us with the realization that He is God and we can surrender our cares into His hands. We can pray with our hearts.

THE COOKIE CUTTER WON'T WORK

When I was in college, I participated in a Christian organization that was a great source of fellowship and encouragement to me. But one semester our group was asked to be part of a pilot project for a publisher that was trying out a new devotional pattern and resource for students. Each month we were given a new batch of material consisting of a page for each day of the month. Each day the format was the same: there was a passage from the Bible to study, using a set of questions and notes that were provided, and a process for praying about the implications of the text for our lives. There were those in our group for whom the material was like water on parched ground. But it was agonizingly difficult for me. Perhaps I didn't have the attention span to stay on task, or maybe the approach wasn't sufficiently appealing to cause me to continue with it day after day. However, when I went to our group meetings and heard the others talk so glowingly of their experience with this devotional structure, I felt like a spiritual misfit. I felt that I would suffocate if I didn't get out of that program!

Perhaps you have had similar experiences when a youth counselor or influential spiritual leader attempted to fit you into his or her mold by promoting a devotional discipline or a prayer pattern that he or she thought everyone ought to use. But you found that it didn't fit you. You may have felt like a spiritual failure when the approach left you cold. Or perhaps you forced yourself into compliance and ended up in bondage to a system as if it were an end in itself, rather than a means of living in connection with the living Christ. The point is that there is no cookie-cutter approach when it comes to prayer.

IMPORTANT REMINDERS FROM SAINTS OF THE PAST

Many of the great spiritual directors over the centuries had a special sensitivity when it came to appreciating the differences among people and guiding each person to the practices and approaches that would be most helpful for spiritual nourishment. With consideration and wisdom they encouraged people to be themselves before God.

Abbe de Tourville wrote that "one does not become holy by copying others but by making good use of what is truly part of oneself." He instructed people to pray in ways that were most conducive to them.

When your soul begins to feel more at home, it will be easier to find out what is usually for you the quickest way of coming into the close and living presence of Jesus Christ. You will then be able to develop this special bent with greater certainty and will gradually discover the endless variety of ways in which it can grow. You will thus have cleared your path. For nothing is more individual to each soul than the form of its intimacy with our Lord.[4]

Thomas à Kempis, writing in the 1400s, counseled those with whom he worked that it was important for them to have flexibility and an experimental attitude when it came to cultivating their relationship with God.

> Tailor-make your private devotions;
> some exercises suit certain persons better than others.
> The season makes a difference, too;
> and a working day may be different from special sacred days.
> Times of temptation require a devotional discipline
> different from that of times of peace and quiet.
> A pensive mood requires a different kind of exercise than does a
> joyful state of mind.[5]

Not only are persons to find their own "voice" when it comes to prayer and devotion, but the best spiritual directors urged us to show others the same consideration as well. To do otherwise would be closer to "cloning" than making disciples.

Dom Augustine Baker, who lived in the 1600s, cautioned that those who serve as spiritual friends or pastors need to be perceptive about the personality and need of each person whom they teach or guide:

> Always remembering that his office is not to teach his own way,
> nor indeed any determinate way of prayer, etc., but to instruct his disciples how they may themselves find out the way proper to them, by observing themselves what does good and what causes harm to their spirits; in a word, that "instructor" is only God's usher, and must lead souls in God's way and not his own.[6]

Evelyn Underhill picked up on this same theme in an address to a group of English clergy in the 1920s. She noted that we who are pastors must first find our own best way to nurture and express our friendship with God, and then we need to be careful to treat other persons with similar thoughtfulness.

> We shall find, when we look into our own souls, or study those with whom we have to deal, that there is an immense variation among them; both in aptitude, and in method of approaching God. We shall discover that only certain devotional books and certain devotional symbols and practices truly have meaning for us; whilst others will appeal to other men . . . the first thing we have to find out is the kind of practice that suits *our* souls:—yours, not someone else's, and now, at this stage of its growth. You have to find and develop the prayer that fully employs you and yet does not over-strain you; the prayer in which you are quite supple before God; the prayer that refreshes, braces and expands you, and is best able to carry you over the inevitable fluctuations of spiritual level and mood. But in thus making up your minds to use that method towards which you are most deeply

and persistently attracted, and to feed your souls on the food that you can digest, you must nevertheless retain an entire and supple willingness to give others, if desirable, a quite different diet, encourage in them another sort of practice. More than this, you must for their sakes try to learn all you can about other methods than your own.[7]

Underhill insisted that clergy are the very last persons on earth who can afford to latch onto one method of prayer or devotion and try to make that mandatory for everyone else. We need to realize that those methods to which we may become so attached are actually changeable and only have value when they are means of expressing worship and deepening communion with God. Methods need to be held with a loose grip so that if they cease being effective as means for opening us to the grace of God, we can lay them aside in preference for approaches that are more helpful.

GOD ACCOMMODATES TO OUR DIFFERENCES

My wife, Jo, and I have four children. Each is, as you would expect, singularly unique and, thus, strikingly different from all the others in the family. As parents, we delight in this array of personalities when we gather for meals. When our children were young, I was sometimes away on business for a few days. Before returning home, I would search for just the right gift to bring home to each child. There were times that this hunt would take an inordinate amount of time because I wanted to find just the right thing for each one. I would not choose the same thing for Nate that I selected for Katie; and what I selected for Josh would not be the same as the present that I picked out for Wes. I took into account their ages, interests, and temperaments. Gift buying was a way of treasuring individuality. It was evident in my way of relating to our children too. The conversations that I had with each were noticeably different because I accommodated myself to the interests, ages, and personalities of each one. Here's the point, to adapt a saying of Jesus: If I, being evil, know how to give good gifts to my children, how much more does our Heavenly Father treasure our differences and find ways of honoring our uniqueness? He shows it by the wonderful ways that He accommodates himself to us. That there are so many different paths into prayer, styles of devotion, or types of Christian spirituality should not surprise us at all. God cherishes our uniqueness.

WAYS OF SPENDING TIME IN GOD'S PRESENCE

In their book _Varieties of Prayer_, Margaret Poloma and George Gallup Jr. published the results of a follow-up study of the 88 percent who had responded to a Gallup Survey indicating that they prayed on a regular basis.[8] The approach was simple. People who said they prayed were asked, "When you pray, describe what you normally do." Responses varied in fascinating ways. About 84 percent of the respondents said that when they prayed, they talked to God conversationally, expressing in their own words their requests for forgiveness or for divine assistance in some situation. Prayer of petition was important for 42 percent of the surveyed. They described how they asked God for the material things they needed. About 50 percent of the respondents reported that they recited prayers they memorized. "Meditative prayer" was important for 21 percent who indicated that they used a prayer book or the Book of Psalms in the Bible. Still others (52 percent) described how, when they prayed, they sought to be quiet in God's presence, to feel or be aware of His nearness, trying to listen for what God might want to say to them or just spending time worshiping and adoring God. People prayed in so many different ways.

That research inspired me to try a similar experiment with students in my spiritual formation classes, or with people who attended the retreats I led. I invited them to tell me how they prayed. Responses were varied and instructive. Eventually I developed my list into the following workshop exercise. As you read the items, make note of the practices you normally use, but also pay attention to other ideas that attract you and with which you may want to experiment.

When you pray, do you typically . . .

- ☐ read prayers from a book or from the Psalms?
- ☐ write your prayers?
- ☐ recite prayers you have memorized?
- ☐ follow an outline or pattern in your prayer time?
- ☐ talk to God, spontaneously, in your own words?
- ☐ express your feelings to God?
- ☐ intercede by entering empathetically into the feelings of others and bearing these feelings to God in prayer?
- ☐ intercede by talking to God about others' needs?
- ☐ intercede silently by visualizing the other person in Christ's presence?
- ☐ intercede for others while looking at their photographs?
- ☐ intercede for others with the use of a "prayer list"?
- ☐ spend time just "feeling" the presence of God?
- ☐ spend time quietly thinking about God?
- ☐ listen in silence for what God wants to say?
- ☐ pray a phrase or verse from Scripture in order to focus your attention and rest in God's presence?
- ☐ imagine Christ present with you, or visualize yourself as present

with Him in some gospel scene, and let that lead into conversational prayer with Christ?

☐ read a passage of scripture and try to allow God to show you how it relates to or applies to your life?

☐ read from a devotional source that raises your thoughts to God and helps you think about His attributes and qualities and stimulate your worship?

☐ pray over your day's schedule, offering persons and situations to God in anticipatory prayer, and seek God's help in ordering your priorities?

☐ read a selection from a devotional source that relates stories about how real people have experienced God in their circumstances, using it as a "faith lift"?

☐ "daydream" or follow a stream of consciousness in God's presence, allowing it to take you "wherever" as you open yourself to God— all the way from confession of sins, asking for help, or receiving creative ideas?

☐ think about something in a focused way, in God's presence, perhaps with pen in hand?

☐ use symbols in your place of prayer (for example, a lit candle, open Bible, picture, cross, or worship center of some sort)?

☐ sing, play a musical instrument, or listen to music during your time of prayer?

☐ keep a spiritual journal or prayer diary?

☐ set aside time during prayer in order to reflect deliberately over your day, in order to see how God has been (or may have wanted to be) at work?

☐ set aside time for self-examination into your attitudes, actions, or thoughts that are hindering your relationship with God?

☐ "practice the presence of God" during the day by frequent interior conversations with Him?

☐ find that there are frequent moments through the day when your thoughts turn to God and you are conscious of His presence in you?

☐ organize your schedule so that there are fixed times throughout the day when you remind yourself to lift your heart to God in prayer?

☐ "pray with your body" by using posture (kneeling, lying prostrate, etc.), actions (dancing or movement), or gestures (palms opened, arms lifted, etc.) as a means of prayerful expression to God?

- ☐ sometimes use voluntary denial of an otherwise normal function (eating, watching TV, sweets, etc.) for the sake of spiritual focus and prayer?
- ☐ walk/jog/play in order to place yourself in the "path" of God who lifts your spirit through the beauty of creation?
- ☐ listen to audiotapes of scripture selections, as you drive, work, or rest?
- ☐ use your Bible computer software to prayerfully interact with Scripture?
- ☐ read/sing from the hymnal in order to drink in the message that comes through the poetic imagery as a means of being with God?

STAYING CONNECTED

Recognizing how vast are the possibilities for spending time in God's presence has a way of helping us appreciate our uniqueness and to be mindful of how our prayer-preferences and devotional styles may change according to our needs at different stages and seasons of life. The important thing about deepening intimacy with God is to find those ways that are most conducive to "being ourselves" with God and to utilize as many of those practices as we can in order to stay in conscious connection with Him throughout the day.

God loves us and delights in our distinctiveness. Prayer is His gift to us, but it is also a decision we make to be with Him. As we give the relationship time, our friendship can grow. The more we open ourselves to God, the more we discover about God and what He wants to be for us. God uses prayer to bring out His best in us so that He can use us to bring about His best for others.

Notes

1. William A. Barry, S.J., *God and You: Prayer as Personal Relationship* (New York: Paulist Press, 1987), 17-18.

2. I am indebted to my colleague, Robert Mulholland, for this phrase. See his helpful book by the same title, published by the Upper Room.

3. "Polemical" and "confrontational" prayer are described helpfully in Bruce Duncan's book *Pray Your Way* (London: Darton, Longman and Todd, 1994), 114.

4. Abbe De Tourville, *Letters of Direction: Thoughts on the Spiritual Life* (London: Dacre Press, 1961), 38.

5. Thomas à Kempis, *The Imitation of Christ*, paraphrased by Donald E. Demaray (Grand Rapids: Baker, 1982), 43.

6. Quoted in Jerome M. Neufelder and Mary C. Coelho, eds., *Writings on Spiritual Direction by Great Christian Masters* (Minneapolis: Seabury Press, 1982), 27.

7. Evelyn Underhill, *Concerning the Inner Life* (New York: E. P. Dutton and Company, 1926), 39-41.

8. Margaret M. Poloma and George H. Gallup Jr., *Varieties of Prayer: A Survey Report* (Philadelphia: Trinity Press International, 1991).

For Further Reading

Barry, William A., S.J. *God and You: Prayer as Personal Relationship*. New York: Paulist Press, 1987.

Brown, Patricia D. *Paths to Prayer: Finding Your Own Way to the Presence of God*. San Francisco: Josey-Bass, 2003.

Duncan, Bruce. *Pray Your Way*. London: Darton, Longman and Todd, 1995.

Johnson, Reginald. *Your Personality and the Spiritual Life*. Gainesville, Fla.: Center for Applications of Psychological Type, Inc., 1999.

_____. *Learning to Pray Again: A Multimedia, 2-CD, Short Course on Prayer*. Nashville: Cokesbury, 2004.

Michael, Chester P., and Marie C. Norrisey. *Prayer and Temperament: Different Prayer Forms for Different Personality Types*. Charlottesville, Va.: The Open Door, 1984.

Poloma, Margaret M., and George H. Gallup Jr. *Varieties of Prayer: A Survey Report*. Philadelphia: Trinity Press International, 1991.

Thomas, Gary. *Sacred Pathways: Discovering Your Soul's Path to God*. Grand Rapids: Zondervan, 2000.

Jan Johnson is a writer, speaker, and spiritual director. She holds a B.A. in Christian education from Ozark Christian College and is pursuing her D.Min. in Ignatian Spirituality and Spiritual Direction at the Graduate Theological Foundation. Ms. Johnson has authored numerous magazine articles and 13 books, including *Enjoying the Presence of God, When the Soul Listens,* and *Savoring God's Word* (from which this chapter is loosely adapted with the permission of NavPress). She is also a frequent speaker at retreats and conferences. She is married to Greg, who works for a financial software company. Their two children, Jeff and Janae, are young adults who attend college and volunteer at an inner-city youth center. She may be contacted at www.janjohnson.org.

6
Meditating on Scripture
Jan Johnson

❧ As you thumb through this book, you may wonder why a chapter on Scripture meditation is included. Surely meditation is a frill. As a pastor, you already have too much to do—why add another practice to your spiritual life?

Let me begin with a secondary benefit first. While you want to minister with the heart of Christ, there are days when you shock yourself. There's the time you got up to speak on a platform—preaching a sermon, perhaps just making announcements—and it seemed so routine that you felt as if you could turn around and watch yourself up there. You got through it by staying on automatic pilot. Or there's the time you were talking with the dear woman in the church who'd just had a stroke. Even though she was telling you something intensely personal, you found your eyes fascinated with how part of her face drooped so much. How could you, a kind caring person, be so distracted in a moment that should have called forth compassion from you?

When the to-do list is overwhelming or we are peopled out, the mind, heart, and body lose focus. It becomes easy to go through the motions, to show up but leave the deepest parts of ourselves at home. We do good deeds but feel annoyed at the people we're serving and wish we were soaking in a hot tub instead. How unpracticed we are at focusing on someone and staying in that moment. Meditating on Scripture provides this retraining.

Scripture meditation also retrains the divided heart as well as the distracted mind. Most of the time the heart is torn between cooperating with God and serving what psychiatrist Gerald May calls the "false trinity": power, possessions, and human relationships.[1] We want to humble ourselves, but we also want to make sure we get the credit we deserve. We want to submit to the other person, but also to have our own way. We want to respect others' choices, but also to convince them to comply with ours. Yet when Scripture meditation has allowed the words, phrases, and images of Scripture to dance in our heads for days, we're more likely to remain so connected with God that we are changed at the heart level. We actually want to be humble or love our enemy. Exercises such as meditation allow God to ravish us with the divine personality and draw us toward the Kingdom life that understands that humility makes life so much easier, so free of striving, competing, and proving ourselves. Instead of running on reserves, we function in the power of the kingdom of God and pay close attention to God in this moment.

Yet such focusing ability and singleheartedness pale compared to the chief benefit of Scripture meditation—encountering God in a personal way every day of our lives. By immersing ourselves in interaction with God, we have a sense of our lives intermingling with Christ's life. These daily exchanges with God change us little by little. Without them our daily cries revert to, "I must have . . . I must be . . . I must achieve . . ." Exercises such as Scripture meditation cultivate the heart and guard it from those stubborn habits that woo us—laziness, grouchiness, and self-absorption (Prov. 4:23; 23:19). Interacting with Jesus in such an uncalculated way equips us with the ability to talk, serve, and react as Jesus did. In meditation, those winsome ways are caught rather than just taught.

TRAINING, NOT TRYING

Spiritual disciplines function in the formation of our soul by giving us a way to be transformed into Christlikeness through something other than trying to be good. This straining to be righteous quickly becomes centered on ourselves, and we spend most of our time being disappointed in ourselves and focused on reforming ourselves. Spiritual disciplines (or exercises or strategies), in contrast, help us connect with God as many moments of the day as possible.

For example, I used to read 1 Cor. 13:4-8 and beat myself up. Was I patient? No. Was I kind? No. Did I envy? Yes. I failed the tests every time. But while meditating on the passage, it occurred to me that since God is love, the descriptions of love were also descriptions of God. Because God is love, God is then patient and kind. God does not envy or boast. God is not proud or rude or self-seeking or easily irritated. God doesn't keep a record of wrongs. God doesn't delight in evil but rejoices in truth. No matter what, God always protects, always trusts, always hopes, and always perseveres. God never fails.

As I tasted these words over and over, I felt so grateful that God doesn't keep a record of my wrongs, that God isn't rude to me, no matter how discourteously or braggadociously I behave. I felt such love for this God who always protects, always trusts, always hopes, and always perseveres. I am often cynical, but God always hopes. I am suspicious, but God always trusts. I sensed my outlook shifting. After meditating on this passage one day, I decided not to have a Mom-talk with my then 21-year-old son about a rude remark he'd made. I decided that instead I would continue to love and encourage him. I followed through, and a few days later, the opportunity arose to mention—lightly and casually—the more desirable behavior. He smiled and said, "Oh. OK." How different our interchange was because I'd spent a few moments being intrigued by God's personality of love.

This is how connecting with God leads to our transformation. You do the connecting while God does the perfecting. This concept is detailed in the text of Josh. 1:8: "Do not let this Book of the Law depart from your mouth; meditate on it day and night, *so that you may be careful to do* everything written in it. Then you will be prosperous and successful" (italics mine). When you regularly meditate on God's laws of goodness, something changes inside you and you more naturally become careful to do them. You want to do them. Goodness flows instead of being forced.

If you wish, go back over the second paragraph in this section that begins with "For example, . . ." Read those paraphrased words from 1 Cor. 13 a few times. Sit in these ideas. Shut your eyes. What is God saying to you today about himself?² Don't worry at this point about whether you're doing this right. Just try it out.

MEDITATION: UNFAMILIAR TERRITORY

Scripture meditation is one of the classic spiritual disciplines used for centuries by the people of God. Celebrating the Passover involved such intense meditation that Hebrew families even wore dress-ups (traveling clothes) and used props (unleavened bread) to relive the account in Scripture. Mary, the mother of Jesus, pondered Scripture and treasured it to the point that when she sang out the Magnificat, it was full of the Scripture she had spent years pondering (Luke 1:46-55; 1 Sam. 2:1-10).

But Scripture meditation is not well practiced among modern, Western Christians, and many don't know how to do it. And Scripture doesn't tell us how to meditate. That's because Middle Easterners in Old and New Testament times knew how to meditate, just as they knew how to fast. As a result, no instructions for fasting or meditation were given. So we do what seekers of God have always done: we talk to others who are practiced in fasting and meditation to find out how to do them. While many methods exist, two have been used throughout history. One is spiritual reading—lectio divina—which is explained in chapter 7, "The Word Became Text: The Nature of Spiritual Reading" by Robert Mulholland. The other method involves reading a narrative passage, usually a gospel scene, and imagining it. This was popularized by Catholic reformer Ignatius of Loyola (1491—1556), and we'll examine this method below.

Besides, Scripture meditation may not be so unfamiliar. If you've enjoyed word studies or word pictures, you've dabbled in Scripture meditation. For example, it's easy to meditate on the idea of being "stayed" in Isa. 26:3 (KJV): "Thou wilt keep him in perfect peace, whose mind is stayed on thee: because he trusteth in thee." The original Hebrew word for "stayed" is a word used to describe the way a rope is fastened to a tent peg. Imagine powerful Middle Eastern winds pulling on the ropes that fastened down the enormous tents in which Israelite herdsmen lived. Their clothes may have flapped furiously in the wind, but the tent peg (and therefore the tent) stayed in place because of the "staying" power of that rope. In the same way, when we experience tornado-like chaos in our lives, our goal is to keep our minds stayed on God.

IGNATIAN-STYLE MEDITATION: THE "MOVIE METHOD"

Try this taste of this imaginative meditation:

Step 1: Read this passage slowly.

It was just before the Passover Feast. Jesus knew that the time had come for him to leave this world and go to the Father. Having loved his own who were in the world, he now showed them the full extent of his love. The evening meal was being served, and the devil had already prompted Judas Iscariot, son of Simon, to betray Jesus. Jesus knew that the Father had put all things under his power, and that he had come from God and was returning to God; so he got up from the meal, took off his outer clothing, and wrapped a towel around his waist. After that, he poured water into a basin and began to wash his disciples' feet, drying them with the towel that was wrapped around him. He came to Simon Peter, who said to him, "Lord, are you going to wash my feet?" Jesus replied, "You do not realize now what I am doing, but later you will understand." . . .

When he had finished washing their feet, he put on his clothes and returned to his place. "Do you understand what I have done for you?" he asked them. "You call me 'Teacher' and 'Lord,' and rightly so, for that is what I am. Now that I, your Lord and Teacher, have washed your feet, you also should wash one another's feet. I have set you an example that you should do as I have done for you" *(John 13:1-7, 12-15)*.

Step 2: Reread the passage above more slowly, but first read the questions below to ponder as you read.

How do you feel as you observe Jesus? Imagine the disciples' shock as Jesus dropped His outer clothing and wrapped only a towel around His waist. How would you have felt if you had been a disciple? Can you picture Jesus preparing the water and finding the towel?

What do you think His face might have looked like as He washed each one's feet?

What do you think His face looked like as He washed Judas's feet? How do respond to Jesus' serving His enemy? To Jesus' claim when not in safe territory? To Jesus' love for His false friend?

What do you experience as Jesus interacts with Peter who, as usual, is a little over the top? Do you think He laughed as He responded to Peter? If not, how do see Jesus responding?

Now read the passage above. Become a fly on the wall. If God leads you to assume the identity of one of the persons, do so. (Don't pick the person yourself, but let that choice come to you.)

Step 3: Sit in this scene a few more minutes. Then ask yourself, What invitation is this passage offering you? To welcome a betrayer? To be vulnerable because you know who you are and you are confident that God will make certain your needs are met? (Jesus "knew that the Father had put all things under his power, and that he had come from God and was returning to God" [v. 3].)

Be honest about Jesus' vulnerability. Is this challenge to attempt such vulnerable service scary, threatening, requiring too much risk or too much work, or beyond your faith? Or is it something you want to try more of? Don't worry if these questions are too difficult to answer. God may simply be inviting you to ponder them.

Step 4: Respond to God in prayer. Say to God whatever you need to say in response to this passage.

EXAMINING THE METHOD

The above sequence invited you to step into a scene from Scripture. Because this method of meditation invites you to relive an event in Scripture, it can be called the "movie method" or picture prayer. If prompted by God, we become one of the characters, seeing the story unfold from that character's viewpoint. The aim is to enter the biblical narrative to more fully participate in Jesus' mind, heart, and work. With this method, "it is wise to ask the Spirit to guide the use of our inner resources so that through them we may hear whatever word God wishes to speak."[3]

Consider how this way of approaching Scripture may be very different from what you're used to.

Not Bible study. While you are no doubt skilled at gathering historical and cultural information about the text and examining the context and parallel passages, Scripture meditation asks you to leave that in the background. It is still important because Bible study acts as Step 1 to meditation, which is Step 2. "Scripture study is an essential supplement to ongoing lectio but is not directly involved in this process."[4] For example, knowing the context of the above scene tells you that Judas was about to betray Jesus. It tells you how long Jesus had been with the disciples and that there had been resentments about who would be honored. Knowing the culture and customs about foot washing is helpful. All of that background helps us meditate with more discernment. Books such as Alfred Edersheim's *The Life and Times of Jesus the Messiah* immerse you in the culture of Bible times.

Not application. To meditate on a passage is not to ask oneself, "Where in my work, family life, finances, health, or relationship with God do I need the principles of this passage?" This is an excellent question to ask, but meditation is different. You stop thinking so hard and wait for God to speak. The closest you come to application might be asking: "How does this passage intersect with my life?" But you're asking God, not yourself.

Both study and application are primarily left-brain activities where you connect the dots between facts or between the principle of the passage and how you drive your car. But meditation is right-brained and intuitive. You quiet yourself but remain attentive. You hear what you need to know either during the quiet of meditation or later. On the other hand, you will not be overwhelmed with nonstop flashes of insight just because meditation is more intuitive. Meditation is a skill, and it takes time to let go of all the voices in your mind telling you what to do.

Not personality-driven. Perhaps you've decided that meditation is for those who "live in their head." You have little intuition or imagination—you're an active doer. Consider that the most meditative person in Scripture—David, the psalm writer—was also a Rambo-like warrior. This ultimate doer was also a ponderer. Consider also that gardening and driving are excellent venues for pondering, once the skill is learned.

CONTRARY TO MODERN IDEAS

Perhaps you think that since you may not have been taught to meditate in seminary, it can't be important. It's true that meditation seems unfamiliar because it is at odds with the views of modernity (ideas and events permeating roughly A.D. 1500 to 2000). The last 500 years have largely been about conquest and control. For example, two continents and many diseases have been conquered. Through the development of the machine, we found the best, most efficient ways to get things done. In this age of analysis, matter and ideas have been dissected and examined endlessly. All this progress has created an infatuation with newness so that we routinely throw off old ideas, thinking that newer ones are usually better. Such "progress" also makes us extremely objective, so that we replace "mysteries with comprehension, ignorance with information."[5]

While many features of modernity have helped us, they have also invaded and shaded the biblical view of faith. Spirituality is now about conquering and efficiency. We pray in order to get results, forgetting that prayer is about getting more of God within ourselves. We search for machinelike ways to make our "time with God" productive. The mysteries of God are solved in apologetics books. The subjective parts of Scripture—the poetry and imagery of the prophets—are less easily charted, and so we don't read them as much. Yet God allowed much of Scripture to be written in poetic, mysterious terms. Even Paul's Epistles include paradoxes such as this one: "to know this love that surpasses knowledge" (Eph. 3:19). If this love surpasses knowledge, it cannot be known. So why bother "knowing" unknowable love? Yet grasping this unfathomable love of God is the main point of the prayer.

The products of meditation (hearing God, transformation into Christlikeness) are not precise and, therefore, difficult to grade ourselves on. Simply letting the Scripture text speak is not quick. It involves waiting, an honored activity in Scripture, but shunned by us productive moderns.

In this glow of modernity, such biblical exercises as meditation have been overlooked. The two primary methods of meditation have been used for centuries, and so to some, they seem outdated and useless. Consider the opposite may be true. Don't credible methods stand the tests of time? Aren't they learned from standing on the shoulders of spiritual giants? Over hundreds of years, people have tested the spirits and found these methods credible and helpful.

Imaginary Troubles

Some Christians are bothered that this style of meditation makes use of the imagination, but Jesus stimulated listeners' imaginations by using parables, images, and word pictures. He asked listeners to picture buried treasure, an unjust judge, a mugging on the Jericho road, a house ludicrously built on sand, and someone swallowing a camel-inhabited drink without noticing it (after having fussed over there being a tiny gnat in it). Did the apostle John see heaven through his physical eyes or through the interior eyes of his retrained imagination (Rev. 10:1; 15:1; 18:1; 19:11; 20:1; 21:1-2)? We don't know, but for 2,000 years Christians have used their imaginations to picture John's images from the pages of Revelation.

It's true that imagination has been a source of false prophecy and idol worship (Ezek. 13:2; Isa. 65:2), but what if imagination's potential for misleading us were reconfigured by the mind of Christ, which Paul claims we possess (1 Cor. 2:16)? Armed with stories, images, and hopes drawn from God's history with the people of God (as Christ's mind was), imagination can become a penetrating force."[6] The problem is that we have let our imagination go to the devil, and so we find it easy to imagine strangling a relative or committing adultery in the heart (Matt. 5:27-28).

It's also true that some might distort the intended meaning of the

Scripture in imaginative meditation. But people distort every spiritual discipline—Bible study, prayer, fasting, and so on. That doesn't mean we ignore these disciplines, but we learn how to meditate from those who have done it well. We meditate on scriptures we have studied because when we're familiar with their historical, linguistic, and cultural details, we're less likely to distort them.

As disciples of Jesus, we are responsible to let our imagination be retrained for God's purposes. We ask God to retrain every part of ourselves—tongue, thoughts, hearts, feet, lips, arms, and knees (1 Pet. 3:10; 2 Cor. 10:5; James 4:8; Eph. 6:15; Col. 3:8; Heb. 12:12) so that we are transformed into Christlikeness. We're also to renew our minds (Rom. 12:2), which includes our imagination.

PRACTICAL OBSTACLES

The most common problem in meditation seems to be quieting oneself. While most of life involves being transfixed with a book, tuned into the radio, or mesmerized by a TV show, meditation thrives on silence.

As creatures of such a noisy culture, we do one of two things when we sit quietly. One is that we fall asleep. If this happens to you, God bless you. You must have needed to sleep—most pastors do. The other common response is that your mind will race as you make a mental list of things you have to do and people you have to contact. In that case, keep pad and paper nearby and jot down to-do items that distract you. As you list each errand to run or person to call, consciously release it to God.

Pray about issues that distract your thoughts. Dietrich Bonhoeffer counsels,

> Our thoughts are likely to wander and go their own way toward other persons or to some events in our life. Much as this may distress and shame us again and again, we must not lose heart and become anxious, or even conclude that meditation is really not something for us. When this happens it is often a help not to snatch back our thoughts convulsively, but quite calmly to incorporate into our prayer the people and events to which our thoughts keep straying and thus in all patience return to the starting point of the meditation.[7]

Don't scold yourself, but gently include your distracting thoughts in your prayer.

Choosing time of day. "Choose the time of the day when we are most alert, least distracted, least tired, most well-rested, and without outside pressure."[8] Most people recommend you do this first thing when you arise. While this is optimal, it doesn't work for many people and forcing ourselves to do it makes it worse. If you're not a morning person and it doesn't work for you, choose another time when you are relaxed and clear-headed.

Choosing Scripture text. The process of hunting to discover the text for the day is distracting, so follow any sort of plan. You may use a recommended list (such as a lectionary) or stay with a theme (Jesus' healings) or simply work through a book of the Bible. Ten verses or less a day is sufficient. Your goal is not to get through the book but to connect with God.

Consider the centrality of the Gospels. Francis de Sales, well practiced in meditation, advised, "I especially counsel you to practice mental prayer, the prayer of the heart, and particularly that which centers on the life and passion of our Lord. By often turning your eyes on him in meditation, your whole soul will be filled with him. You will learn his ways and form your actions after the pattern of his."[9] Meditating on Gospel passages helps you get to know the character and personality of Jesus. Then you're more likely to know what Jesus would say or do in any given situation in your life.

Be open to shifting your plans when needed. For four years, I moved through Old Testament prophets with great joy. But the summer my mother died, I switched to meditating through the Gospel of Mark. I needed familiar passages that kept Jesus front and center in my mind.

In the beginning, choose texts that answer the needs of your soul, especially your places of brokenness. For example, those sensing they don't truly believe God loves them may want to meditate on passages that mention God delighting in us:

Zeph. 3:17: "The LORD your God is with you, he is mighty to save. He will take great delight in you, he will quiet you with his love, he will rejoice over you with singing."

Ps. 18:19: "He brought me out into a spacious place; he rescued me because he delighted in me."

Making it up. When you meditate and seem to hear insights, you may wonder, Am I putting words in God's mouth? Am I making this up? Your first line of defense is to see if what comes to you flows with Scripture. God doesn't say anything that's out of sync with scriptural commands (to kill or exploit someone) or divine nature (God is full of integrity and mercy). But close behind that line of defense is to figure out if it's the kind of thing you always seem to say, usually a dysfunctional voice at that. Do you usually hear God scolding you? Set it aside. Do you usually hear God scolding a certain person in your church? Set it aside.

Those of us who have taught Scripture a lot tend to hear the sermon outline of our favorite teacher from 15 years ago. While that was probably excellent teaching, set it aside.

If you think you might be controlling the meditation, ask yourself: Am I writing the script or receiving it? Am I able to be surprised by what comes to me? It can be difficult to surrender the control to God, but it's worth it because we will hear what we really need to know in life. You may even be afraid to hear what God would say to you, but try it. It's an exciting adventure into real interaction with God, and "we will never be 'in charge' in prayer if it is real."[10]

If you find yourself forcing something artificial, admit it and set it aside. Then ask God, "What else?" If nothing else comes, hold on to the original idea, but wait. You will know the authenticity of it by its fruit (Matt. 7:20), by what it leads you to do. You can also test its authenticity by running it by someone wiser than you in the Lord—a mentor or spiritual director. Or you may wish to journal about it and read it later to test it yourself. Don't be discouraged by this. This is good training in learning to hear the Shepherd's voice (John 10:3-4), and this process will make your ears sharper.

If you continually come up with clever insights that are probably yours, work at grounding yourself in the details of the setting and culture of the passage. Focus on the kind of work shepherds did and what the grasslands Jacob slept in were like. These help you let go of your agenda. Details will immerse you in the text and keep you focused.

If you get used to meditating on Scripture, you'll find you can spot Bible teachers who meditate. Their teaching is so different because they have such easy familiarity with the flow of the passage. At that point, you will be tempted to meditate just so you can be a more effective teacher! But my guess is that if you do that, you'll start longing for your personal encounters with Jesus and go back to being drawn into passages just for the sake of tasting and seeing that He is good. And that will be good.

Notes

1. Gerald May, *Addiction and Grace* (San Francisco: Harper and Row, Publishers, 1988), 32.

2. Another variation is to take the phrase "speaking the truth in love" (Eph. 4:15) and substitute the words from 1 Cor. 13 for "love." So ask God, what would it look like to speak the truth with patience? With kindness? Without rudeness? Without pride? Without keeping a record of wrongs? What if church leaders routinely did such a meditation before any meeting? What would change?

3. Marjorie Thompson, "Praying with Scripture," *Weavings*, Vol. V, No. 3 (May/June 1990), 39.

4. Norvene Vest, *Gathered in the Word* (Nashville: Upper Room Books, 1996), 11.

5. Brian McLaren, *A New Kind of Christian* (San Francisco: Jossey-Bass Inc., 2001), 17.

6. John Mogabgab, editor's introduction, *Weavings*, Vol. XII, No. 1 (Jan./Feb. 1997), 2-3.

7. Dietrich Bonhoeffer, *Life Together* (New York: Harper and Row, Publishers, 1954), 85, italics mine.

8. Chester P. Michael and Marie C. Norrisey, _Prayer and Temperament_ (Charlottesville, Va.: The Open Door, 1991), 35.

9. Francis de Sales, _Introduction to the Devout Life_ (New York: Image Books, Doubleday, 1966), 81.

10. Thelma Hall, _Too Deep for Words: Rediscovering Lectio Divina_ (New York: Paulist Press, 1988), 32.

M. Robert Mulholland Jr., Th.D., has been a faculty member at the Wilmore, Kentucky, campus of Asbury Theological Seminary since 1979 and served as vice president and chief academic officer from 1987 to 2002. Besides teaching at McMurry University, he has also been a supply and disbursing officer in the U.S. Navy, a foreman for Scott Paper Co., and the pastor of a recreational ski ministry.

Dr. Mulholland is a nationally known biblical scholar, listed in Who's Who in the Methodist Church, Who's Who in Biblical Studies and Archaeology, and Who's Who in Religion. He is the author of several books on Scripture and spiritual formation, including his books *Shaped by the Word: The Role of Scripture in Spiritual Formation, Invitation to a Journey: A Road Map for Spiritual Formation,* and two volumes on Revelation in the United Methodist Publishing House's Journey Through the Bible series. He has contributed book reviews and articles to many journals, entries to the *Beacon Dictionary of Theology,* the *World Book Encyclopedia,* the *Dictionary of Jesus and the Gospels,* and revisions to Tyndale House's new edition of *The Living Bible.*

As an elder in the Kentucky Conference of the United Methodist Church and a member of the Wesleyan Theological Society and Society of Biblical Literature, Dr. Mulholland is a frequent speaker at Bible and spiritual renewal conferences and serves as a faculty member of the Academy for Spiritual Formation.

He and his wife, Lynn, have two adult children, Jeremy and Tareena.

7
The Word Became Text:
The Nature of Spiritual Reading
M. Robert Mulholland Jr.

🌿 Thomas Merton wrote: "Curiously, the most serious religious people . . . those who constantly read the Bible as a matter of professional or pious duty, can often manage to evade a radically involved dialogue with the book they are questioning."[1]

All too often this is an uncomfortable description of the relationship pastors have with Scripture. The Bible becomes a source of texts for sermons, an object of study in preparation for Bible studies, a resource for Christian education or pastoral counseling, a textbook to be studied like any other, a foundation for constructing an edifice of dogma or doctrine, and even a "weapon" to coerce people into theological or ecclesiastical prisons. The devotional reading of the Bible can become merely a habit, a discipline practiced without any transforming effect upon our life or ministry, a privatized activity that rarely thrusts us into the world with an altered being and a prophetic vision.

Educational preparation for ministry has provided a strong academic frame of reference for our work with the Scripture. Our personal or church libraries provide commentaries and other resources for filling in the gaps in our knowledge and understanding of the text. Thus, subtly, unknowingly, the Bible is often reduced to being one more "tool" in the arsenal of equipment we bring to the task of ministry. Merton's "radically involved dialogue" is often missing in pastors' work with the Scripture.

The lack of a consistent, "radically involved dialogue" with the Scripture may be not only a result of reducing the Scripture to a tool for ministry but also the consequence of a self-referenced approach to ministry. When ministry becomes "our" ministry, when "our" agendas, "our" vision, "our" purpose become the driving force of ministry, the Scripture easily becomes a resource for the confirmation of our self-referenced approach. We do not allow the Scripture to challenge our "self-referencedness," confront our agendas, subvert our vision, or undermine our purpose. Merton reminds us:

"Any serious reading of the Bible means personal involvement in it, not simply mental agreement with abstract propositions. And involvement is dangerous, because it lays one open to unforeseen conclusions."[2] We sense, intuitively, the Scripture can be a threat to the entire self-referenced structure of our life and ministry.

Yet, at the same time, we also sense the Scripture can be a place of liberation from the narrow parameters of our self-referencedness; a source of vision beyond our individualized world of perception; an empowerment for purposes beyond the scope of our parochial interests; and the ground of agendas that can incarnate the very presence of God in the deeply wounded world of our life and ministry. For this to become reality we may need a profound restructuring of our perception of and approach to Scripture.

How can the Bible become a vital center of continual renewal and transformation? How can the Bible be a means of an ever deepening relationship with God and an ever more profound vision of what God is seeking for us to be in the world? I would suggest two inseparably interrelated activities: first, a revolution in our perception of the nature of the Bible; and, second, the regular practice of the classical discipline of spiritual reading, *lectio divina*.

THE NATURE OF THE BIBLE

Perhaps the major problem of the Bible's relative "deadness" in our lives is that the paradigms by which we view it may have limited usefulness. These paradigms are many and are usually interwoven in complex ways: literary, scholarly, canonical, devotional, sociological, modern, and postmodern, just to name a few. While these paradigms have value, the difficulty with such paradigms is they have a way of restricting the Bible to the narrow limits set by the paradigms themselves. For example, although the literary paradigm opens diverse vistas into the multiple genres of the biblical writings and provides lenses with which to view the texts from various angles, it can reduce the Bible to a literary document like any other human writing. The devotional paradigm, although seeking a word from God for our daily life, all too often becomes a privatized and individualized reading that divorces the text from its original context of meaning and reads it through the lenses of our own limited religious experience or the pressing needs of our personal life and ministry. We need a paradigm of approach to the Bible that, while engaging the rich benefits of other paradigms, will provide a metaparadigm that will ground us and the text in the profound reality of God's redemptive and sanctifying presence at the heart of human life as it is lived in any culture at any time.

I believe such a metaparadigm is not only necessary but possible and would suggest the following as a "working model":

The Word became text to provide a place of transforming encounter with God so the Word might become flesh in us in our world.

We are all familiar with the understanding that "the Word became flesh" (John 1:14, NRSV), that God took on human form in the person of Jesus of Nazareth and lived a human life in the midst of a human culture. We are also well aware of the discussions, debates, decrees, and debilitating disruptions within the Christian tradition related to how this human person was, at the same time, fully divine. It is not so much that we have problems understanding humanity, although at times it seems we really understand little of what human existence is all about. Nor is it that we have problems understanding divinity, although we probably understand far less than we think we do. Our real problem is understanding how the divine can be human and how the human can be divine without losing anything of the essence of either.

If we have such irresolvable difficulties with the Word become flesh, is it any wonder we have equally irresolvable difficulties with the Word become text? How can the Scripture be at one and the same time a human document and the Word of God?

1. "The Word Became Text"

This statement is fraught with ambiguity. First, it raises all the issues of inspiration, authority, canon, inerrancy, and infallibility, which, at least since the Enlightenment, have generated much heat but little light. What aspect of the text is human? What is divine? How did the Word become text? Were the writers no more than Dictaphones, were they allowed to exercise any degree of autonomy in the creation of these documents, or are these thoroughly human products somehow imbued with divine presence?

Second, the "Word became text" also raises all the issues of texts. Is the writer the primary locus for the Word that is "entexted"? Or is the text itself the Word manifest? Or is the reader or reading community the matrix in which the text becomes the Word? Where does God fit into all this?

Third, the "Word became text" further raises the issues of interpretation. Do we tease the Word out of the text by the allegorical methods of the early centuries of the Church? Or are the historical-critical methods of the Enlightenment the means for discerning the entexted Word? Or does the Word emerge from the text as a result of a combination of postmodern theories such as reader-response criticism, rhetorical criticism, sociocritical and sociopragmatic hermeneutics, discourse analysis, narrative criticism, semiotics, deconstruction, speech-act theory, or the hermeneutics of metacriticism?

Fourth, the "Word became text" raises the question of the role of "text" in an information age. Is the text an object to be addressed or encountered in order to advance the reader or reading community in some manner? Or is the text a polyvalent nexus constantly presenting ever new facets and nuances that persistently deconstruct all previous understandings and morph new comprehensions?

The "Word became text" draws all these issues and questions into a new paradigm. Just as God mysteriously chose to enter into a human existence, to be limited by all the exigencies of human life, to be misunderstood, rejected, and crucified; so God mysteriously chose to entrust himself to the vagaries of human language and all its similar exigencies for abuse, misunderstanding, and rejection. This is a terribly dangerous undertaking. On the one hand, it allows the text to be used inquisitionally as a bludgeon to manipulate persons and communities into submission to those who wield the power of interpretation. On the other hand, it allows the text to be reduced to nothing but a thoroughly human document like any other and having only that authority and meaning accepted for it by the reading community. However, in a dynamic tension between these two extremes, the "Word became text" also provides an opportunity for the text to become—

2. "A Place of Transforming Encounter with God"[3]

Before we can appreciate the Word become text as a place of transforming encounter with God, we must realize that a noxious danger lies behind the whole hermeneutical endeavor. This danger is rooted in a presumption that the informational dynamic of our culture has magnified. It is the presumption that meaning is communicated primarily, if not wholly, at the cognitive level of human existence and appropriated within the ethos of the reading community. This presumption says if only we could merge the cognitive horizons of the New Testament writers with the cognitive horizon of the contemporary interpreter, then meaning could be communicated for appropriation within the reading community. If we adopt this perception of the transfer of meaning at a cognitive level within a community ethos, then the only parameters we have by which to evaluate our understanding are the parameters established by the community within which we read the text. This is why the Bible tends to be interpreted in the light of diverse contemporary philosophical/cultural/sociological presumptions. We simply read into the text the worldview of our community in order to maintain our cognitive, rational control of the text and authenticate the ethos of our community.

In reaction to this trend, some have tended to stress either the cognitive or the affective level of understanding. On the one hand some say, "If only we can understand the meaning of the text in its original context, then we can transfer that meaning to our life." This presumption, however, is limited by our inability to fully replicate the original context of meaning, and consequently, all too often our own context of meaning is read back into the gaps of our understanding of the original context of the text. On the other hand, some say, "If only we can have what we believe is the same experience the New Testament Church had, then we can automatically understand what they are communicating." However, this presumption results in the varieties of diverse religious experiences becoming the norms of biblical interpretation.

There may be an approach to Scripture that can bridge this gap between cognitive and affective polarities. It is found in a dynamic conjunction of knowledge and vital piety. The cognitive and the affective dimensions of human existence must be conjoined in mutual interdependence if Christians are not to fall into the extremes of sterile intellectualism on the one side or mindless enthusiasm on the other.

How does this relate to the "Word became text" as "a place of transforming encounter with God"? Biblical writers utilized cognitive images from within their perceptual horizon to express the reality of their experience with God, their transforming encounter with the Word and its intrusion into their lives and communities. Their images are cognitive portraits of an affective involvement with the living Word. They convey the "knowledge" of a "vital piety." Now the images—through words and phrases—that the New Testament writers used (and I will limit my illustrations to the portion of the Bible I know best, the New Testament) necessarily contained the conditioning of their perceptual horizon. They were the words and phrases used in the "morning newspaper" in Athens, Jerusalem, Ephesus, or Rome in the first century. However, there was a new and radically different level of communication to the readers who had also entered into the same experience with God.

Aelred Squire succinctly describes this aspect of the communication of meaning. He writes, "It is the man [sic] who lives a certain kind of life who is in a position to understand the doctrine. There are some kinds of knowledge to which experience is the only key."[4]

Paul, I think, expresses this same realization. In 1 Cor. 1—2, he engages in a rather extended discussion on the contrast between the communication of the gospel and the communication of philosophical knowledge. Paul first deals with philosophical wisdom vis-à-vis the proclamation of the gospel (1:18—2:5). Then he writes, "We do speak wisdom" (2:6, NRSV) and next amplifies the nature of the wisdom he speaks (vv. 7-12). It is not a wisdom that correlates with the wisdom of developed human rationality (v. 6). It is a wisdom that has its roots in the experience of the indwelling presence of God through the Holy Spirit (vv. 10-12). Paul closes his description of this wisdom by saying, "We speak of these things [referring back to v. 6] in words not taught by human wisdom but taught by the Spirit, interpreting spiritual things to those who are spiritual" (v. 13, NRSV). He then continues, "Those who are unspiritual do not receive the gifts of God's Spirit, for they are foolishness to them, and they are unable to understand them because they are spiritually discerned. Those who are spiritual discerns all things" (vv. 14-15, NRSV).

It seems although Paul's verbal images—the words he uses in his writing, his proclamation, and his teaching—are images necessarily conditioned by the perceptual horizon of the first-century world, Paul is saying he uses these terms as the only linguistic means available to communicate to his Christian readers the deeper dynamics of their common experience of life shaped by the Word, a life emerging from a transforming encounter with God.

Alan Jones provides another way to look at this dynamic of the "Word became text." He writes, "The journey [inward to God] involves the exploration of images, mythologies, ideas, pictures, in the hope that one or two may become an icon, a window into reality."[5] If we turn this idea around, it illustrates a profound truth about the nature of the "Word became text." What, on the one hand, are icons for those whose lives are intimately involved in the reality portrayed by the text are, on the other hand, but pictures, ideas, myths, and images for those who still stand outside that reality.

I believe this is where the conundrum of biblical interpretation lies. No matter how perfectly we reproduce the perceptual horizon of the New Testament world as the context for understanding the terms and images utilized by the New Testament writers; no matter how objectively and accurately we reproduce the dynamics of human existence in that era; no matter how adequate our cognitive grasp of the life experience of the Christian community, unless we also participate in the experiential reality of life shaped by the living Word, our ultimate understanding of the New Testament writings will be one of seeing images, myths, ideas, and pictures that we can only analyze, "demythologize," or deconstruct in the light of our own experience of human existence.

In Scripture, we can encounter God coming to us, the living Word addressing us, deconstructing our status quo, calling us into transforming encounter, and thrusting us into the world as incarnations of that Word. The Word addresses us in Scripture, however, through human communication, human language. So there is a very real sense in which Scripture is iconographic. Now iconography is rather alien to our Western perception and comprehension. Yet a realization of the iconographic nature of Scripture is essential for our deepest understanding of Scripture as a place of transforming encounter with God.

The writers of Scripture were engaged in a radically new order of being that was shaped by the living Word of God, a life of growing union with

God in love. Of necessity, they were constrained, as we have noted, to use the language of the old order of being, the language of their world, to convey to one another the breadth and length and height and depth of their experience with the Word. In doing this, language becomes iconographic. It becomes a verbal window into the reality of life shaped by the Word, a life in which the Word becomes flesh.

Literary iconography can be illustrated by looking at the New Testament terms for the Church, the community in which the Word becomes flesh in the world. A list of New Testament terms for the Church is mind-boggling. All attempts to give a rational, logical, cognitive organization to these categories fail. We are up against something here that eludes our rational, objective control. The Church is described as city, body, bride, temple, stone, building, house, vineyard, kingdom, nation, family, flock, God's people, army, sons of light, salt, leaven, firstborn, priest, servant, and on and on. Paul Minear described it well:

> No list can exhaust the vivid imaginative power of the NT writers or do justice to the fluidity, vitality, and subtlety of their conceptions. None of the separate titles or pictures can be taken as comprehending the total range of thought. None of them can be reduced to objective, qualifying definitions. These words and pictures are channels of thought rather than receptacles of ideas with fixed meanings. This is due, not alone to the character of the thinking, but also to the qualitative, relational character of the reality being described.[6]

Then Minear focuses precisely upon the truly iconographic nature of the New Testament imagery: "Participation in the life of the church was considered necessary for comprehending the implications of the pictures."[7] In other words, for those who lived within the reality of the new order of being established by God through Jesus and actualized by the presence and work of the Holy Spirit, for the community in which the Word becomes flesh, the multiple, diverse images of the Church became icons through which they perceived and experienced ever new and deeper dimensions of the infinite reality of life shaped by encounter with and response to the living and productive Word of God.

Scripture is iconographic. One of the interesting features of some icons is the farther you look into the picture, the larger things become. Our normal artistic perspective, in which the picture recedes to a vanishing point, is reversed. Icons turn our perspective on its head. When you look at an icon, you discover the point of focus is in you, not "out there" in the picture. You find yourself drawn into a reality, a mystery, that opens out in front of you. Instead of being an independent, objective observer who retains control of the picture, you find the icon conveys an independent, objective reality that encounters you, addresses you, deconstructs your perspective, and draws you into its order of being. This is why, for our Orthodox sisters and brothers, icons are so vital within the community of believers as windows into reality, drawing them into God's new order of being in Christ.

I suggest you begin to think of Scripture iconographically as a model for your basic perception of Scripture. The overload of the self-referenced informational approach of our culture conditions the way we perceive what we read. If we begin to view Scripture iconographically, however, we begin to move into a formational mode. We stand before Scripture, and it opens before us—it addresses us, it decenters us and our status quo, and it draws us into that order of being shaped by the Word. We find ourselves in the presence of the "Word become text." We experience a transforming encounter with God. We begin to discover that all our old structures of identity, meaning, value, purpose, fulfillment, and wholeness are deconstructed. We discover new identity, new meaning, new values, and new purpose. We begin to live in the world, in our relationships, the life of the new order of being in Christ. As we respond to this transforming encounter with God,

3. The Word Becomes "Flesh in Us"

Perhaps an illustration from the world of music will help us integrate what we have been considering with what it means for the Word to "become flesh in us." Think of your favorite symphony (or any other piece of music if you are not a classical music lover). The score for that piece of music is a "text." We may not think of a musical score as a text, but that is exactly what it is. It has its own vocabulary (the various notes: eighth notes, quarter notes, half notes, etc.), its own grammar (the use of the notes on the varied tones within the musical staff), its own syntax (the interplay of the notes and their tones with one another in diverse harmonies and rhythms), its own "cultural" context (the varied key signatures for the varied instrumental families), and its own "sociological" context (the flow of the various tunes, their interplay with other tunes, and their dynamics of intensity). As with any text, it is possible to do a complete and in-depth musicological analysis of any musical text (score). Conceivably a skilled musicologist could analyze a score and accurately describe exactly what the composer was conveying in that score. But would this analysis and, especially, its description convey the reality of the music? Of course not.

A musical text is a literary means for a composer to convey to others the music that has played itself in his or her mind and heart. The "word" of the music becomes "text" in the score. But the "text" is not an end product. The "text" exists to provide a place where musicians can encounter the composer's music itself. In that encounter, if they open themselves to the music, if they allow it to shape their performance, they are, in a sense, transformed as that music becomes part of their musical lives. This, however, is not the composer's end purpose. The composer's purpose in making the music become text is so the musicians may incarnate the music through a performance.

I trust you can now see the implications of the Word becoming text "to provide a place of transforming encounter with God so the Word might become flesh in us." Our encounter with God in the Scripture must never be restricted to an informational exercise. The Word entexted in Scripture must be allowed to penetrate into the depths of our being like a sharp, two-edged sword and disclose the masked motives and hidden agendas of our heart; it must be permitted to lay bare our comfortable, self-referenced status quo, to deconstruct our very being and doing in a transforming encounter with God. Even more, the Word must be allowed to reshape our motives and agendas, to redefine our status quo, to reconstruct our very being and doing in Christlikeness. But we don't ever really know the "meaning" of Scripture until the reality we encounter there becomes incarnate in our life—

4. "In Our World"

John records an almost unbelievable prayer Jesus prays for us: "I ask not only on behalf of these [the eleven disciples], but also on behalf of those who will believe in me through their word, that they may all be one. As you, Father, are in me and I am in you, may they also be in us, so that the world may believe that you have sent me" (John 17:20-21, NRSV). Contrary to many interpretations that claim this text as grounds for theological, doctrinal, or ecclesial conformity, Jesus is praying that we might be in the same relationship with God as He, that we might live in the same kind of loving union with God that characterized His life and ministry. As astounding as this is, however, the purpose for this prayer is even more amazing: "so that the world may believe that you have sent me." Jesus seems to be clearly implying that the world will not believe that God sent Him into the world unless they see the Word become flesh in the lives of His followers!

The world will not be restored to a cleansing, healing, liberating, transforming relationship with God because our theology is accurate, our doctrine pure, our ecclesiology sound, and our proclamation dynamic, as important as these may be. It is the Word becoming flesh in us in our world that will lead the world to believe that God comes into human lives and situations. It is when we become incarnations of the love of God, the mercy of God, the grace of God, and the forgiveness of God for broken, wounded, sin-infected persons that they will know that the Word does indeed become flesh. It is when we become uncomfortable incarnations of the justice of God in the social and economic structures of a corrupt and dehumanizing culture that people will know that the Word does indeed become flesh. As John says in another place, "As he is, so are we in this world" (1 John 4:17, NRSV).

How? How does the Word become text become a place of transforming encounter with God so the Word may become flesh in us in our world?

SPIRITUAL READING[8]

One of the most developed and widely used practices for enabling the Word become text to become the place of transformation we have described is the classical discipline of *lectio divina*. Received by Benedict of Nursia as a rich tradition from the desert mothers and fathers, lectio developed across the centuries as one of the primary means for being transformationally engaged by God for life in the world.

In the classical discipline of lectio divina there are four basic steps to be examined: lectio, meditatio, oratio, and contemplatio. Before we do this, however, it is important to realize that lectio emerged and was practiced in settings where those engaged in it lived in a context of intimacy with God where lives of increasing Christlikeness were expected. This is hardly the circumstance of our life in the world. Thus we need an added introductory and concluding step in our practice of lectio: silencio and incarnatio.

Silencio. If the Scripture is to become a place of transforming encounter with God, we must first adopt an inner attitude of stillness, openness, receptivity, and responsiveness to God in love. We must begin our time with the Word become text by making our self available to God, setting aside our agendas, relinquishing our self-referencedness, willing for God to meet us in the text however God chooses, and committing our self to receiving whatever God brings to us in the text no matter how disturbing or troubling it may be. Silencio is, at its heart, a loving abandonment to God that will allow God to be and do with us whatever God chooses. Don't rush this step. Seek to become as abandoned to God in love as you possibly can.

Lectio. Here we read the text. Choose a small portion; the focus is not on covering large units but plumbing the depths of a small, integral segment. Read the text slowly several times; absorb the text into your mind and heart. It might help, if the nature of the text permits, to place yourself in the role of one or more of the persons in the text and experience the text from those perspectives. Engage your sight, hearing, smell, touch, and even taste as the passage permits. Live in the text as deeply as possible. Take the text into your being. Immerse your being in the text. As you "absorb" the text, take note of how your spirit resonates with the text. Are there moments of delight? Disturbance? Peace? Fear? Sensed loss? Light? Darkness? Decentering? Recentering? Presence? Absence? Resistance? Anger? Joy?

Meditatio. Now we "wrestle" with the text, with the Word become text. If you think of lectio as putting food into your mouth, meditatio is chewing. You ruminate upon the text and how you have been probed by it. What is God saying to you in this text? What engenders those resonances in your spirit? What is the source of your resistance, your fear, your sense of loss? What has been decentered and why? What has been recentered? Throughout your rumination keep your focus on how God is encountering you in the text, how the Word has become text for you.

Oratio. Meditatio should flow seamlessly into oratio—prayer; but this is prayer of a special kind. Up to this point, God has been encountering you in the text if, through abandoned receptivity, you have been allowing the Word become text to be a place of encounter with God. Now you respond to this encounter from your heart. Oratio is no formal, stylized prayer. It is the communication of heart to Heart, spirit to Spirit; it is the outpouring of a person's being to God. In the text God may have probed some deep pool of anger in you, and your oratio is simply screaming out that anger at God. God can handle our anger, and this may be the most real prayer we have ever prayed! In the text God may have touched some hidden sin, and your oratio is tears of repentance. God may have opened a fountain of joy in the text, and your oratio is laughter and singing. God may have been silent in the text, and your oratio is affirming your willingness to wait upon God. A transforming encounter with God is always a two-way relationship, and oratio is the first response of our being to God in that relationship.

Contemplatio. Once we have poured out our heart to God in oratio, we then become still and allow God to implant the Word become text in our heart that the Word might become flesh in us. A powerful image of contemplatio is from Ps. 131: "Truly, I have set my soul in silence and in peace, like a weaned child at its mother's breast."[9] The unweaned child is at its mother's breast for what it needs and wants—milk. The weaned child is the image of abandonment to the mother in love, letting the mother be whatever she wants to be and do whatever she wants to do. Without such radical abandonment to God in love, the Word can never become flesh in us. In contemplatio we may experience deep touches of God or we may experience nothing. Neither is as significant as the contemplatio itself, the nurturing of the soul in a posture of loving abandonment, a yielded availability to God.

Incarnatio. The inner posture of yielded availability must then be carried out into the world of our daily life. If there has been a transformative touch of God upon our life, we must incarnate that reality at the first opportunity. We must allow the Word that has encountered us to become flesh in us, in our life in the world, in our relationships, in the circumstances and situations of our daily existence. A word or phrase from the passage might become the deep inner breathing of our soul as we move through our days.

Here is one practical example of how the Word could become flesh in your daily life. It comes from a very familiar portion of Scripture—the Lord's Prayer.

Jesus teaches us to pray, "Our Father in Heaven" (Matt. 6:9, NRSV). This Word can be the place of a transforming encounter with God; it can structure a whole new mode of being in the world. The first word, "our," indicates that as we initiate openness to God in prayer, we don't do it alone. We come to God within the matrix of all the relationships of our life, real and potential, close and most distant, regular and occasional. We come to God in the context of life in human community, in both the broadest and narrowest sense. The entire human family is caught up in "our," as well as the closer web of our daily relationships and the closest network of friends and family. In the word "our" our relationship with God and our relationships with others are inseparably intertwined.

When we pray "Our *Father*" with integrity, the context of all our human relationships is transformed. Every person encompassed by "our" becomes our sister and brother. Others are no longer valued for the ways they enhance our agenda or devalued for the ways they thwart our purposes. Others can no longer be pawns in our game, objects for the fulfillment of our desires, or enemies to be demonized and destroyed. Every person becomes one whom God loves and for whom God's grace is constantly outpoured. Others are those for whom we are to be the sister or brother in whom God's love and grace touches them. "Our Father" instantly bonds us with God on the one hand and with others on the other hand. If we take these two words, "Our Father," out into our life, if we make them the subtext of every relationship, our relationships will be transformed and the reality of God's dynamic for holistic human relationships will become incarnate in us.

When we pray "Our Father *in heaven*" with integrity, all of life is grounded in a radically alternative mode of being. "In heaven" is not a statement of location; it is the affirmation of God's realm of being in which the "our" can find wholeness of life in loving union with God in relationships with others. "In heaven" affirms a realm whose values, perspectives, and practices are contrary to those of the pervasively self-referenced structures of our culture, a realm that, as Jesus said, is already in our midst (Luke 17:21). If we take these four words, "Our Father in heaven," out into our life, if we make them the subtext of every relationship, the reality of God's realm of shalom and justice will begin to become incarnate in us; the Word will begin to become flesh in us in our world.

Notes

1. Thomas Merton, *Opening the Bible* (Collegeville, Md.: Liturgical Press, 1986), 34.

2. Ibid., 43.

3. Material from this section is drawn, in part, from M. Robert Mulholland Jr., *Shaped by the Word*, rev. ed. (Nashville: Upper Room, 2000).

4. Aelred Squire, *Asking the Fathers* (New York: Paulist Press and Moorehouse-Barlow, 1976), 3.

5. Alan W. Jones, *Journey into Christ* (New York: Seabury Press, 1977), 13.

6. Paul S. Minear, "Church, Idea of," *Interpreters' Dictionary of the Bible*, G. A. Buttrick, ed. (Nashville: Abingdon Press, 1962), 1:616a4.

7. Ibid., 616b.

8. In addition to the practices suggested in this section, cf. "Breaking the Crust," "Wesley's Guidelines for Reading the Scripture," "Obstacles to Spiritual Reading," and "The Practice of Spiritual Reading" (chaps. 10—13) in *Shaped by the Word*.

9. *The Abbey Psalter* (New York: Missionary Society of St. Paul the Apostle, 1981); translation copyright by The Grail, used by special arrangement with William Collins and Sons, Ltd., 1963, published by Paulist Press, Ramsey, N.J.

Neil B. Wiseman, D.Min., after 20 years of ministry as a parish pastor, served for 15 years as academic dean and professor of pastoral development at Nazarene Bible College in Colorado Springs. His other development efforts for ministers include founding and leading Preaching Today, the Minister's Tape Club, Small Church Institute, and *GROW* magazine. He is a graduate of Olivet Nazarene University, Nazarene Theological Seminary, and Vanderbilt Divinity School. Neil and his wife, Bonnie, have two married sons and three grandchildren.

8
Everyday Ministry:
Magnificent Opportunities for Personal Spiritual Growth
Neil B. Wiseman

🕊 YOUR MINISTRY IS A DAILY CELEBRATION OF THE GRACE OF GOD—
never forget it.

I love the wise words of Phillips Brooks, the preacher of Boston fame from an earlier era: "The Christian ministry is the largest field for the growth of a human soul that this world offers. . . . It repeats the experience of Christ's disciples, of whom their Lord was always making larger men."[1]

Great moments, such as Elijah's fiery challenge to Baal's prophets, or unforgettable experiences, such as multiplying a boy's lunch to feed 5,000, are too often considered the most significant shaping forces in a person's spiritual development, especially for a minister. Jesus used epic moments, such as His baptism, crucifixion, and resurrection, to mold His disciples. But He also used ordinary, everyday experiences to call ordinary people from ordinary families to minister to ordinary people in ordinary ways to make an extraordinary impact on their world.

On the basis of the many people he observed around him, President Abraham Lincoln said, "Common-looking people are the best in the world: that is the reason the Lord made so many of them."[2] He was right—the masses are made up of millions of ordinary vanilla persons just like us.

All this ordinariness is the reason I want to make a case for the power of the commonplace, doing the day-by-day ministry so well that it becomes a fertile seedbed for the strongest possible spiritual formation for the minister. What seems ordinary and routine often turns out to be magnificent, even miraculous.

MY ORDINARY JOURNEY OF SPIRITUAL FORMATION

I took my first pastorate—a student charge—quite a few years ago. That started a long journey where the people of God taught me a lot about ministry and even more about how to be a better Christian. So much of my interior development happened as I tried to represent Christ to them.

My start as a pastor took place shortly into my second year in seminary, the first week in November, I believe. Having been married for only two months, I was naively idealistic about ministry and compulsive about life. The place was so ordinary and so full of common people that my seminary classmates loved to call our church Wiseman's mission.

My previous spiritual development had been extremely simple. From infancy I was nurtured by a small, loving branch of God's "forever family" where my young parents were deeply involved. The small congregation worshiped in an ordinary house church located in the middle of a city block in a working-class neighborhood on Detroit's east side. Though my family had northern roots, most church attendees and members were Appalachian transplants who migrated northward for well-paying automobile factory jobs.

The highly unionized environment in our geographic setting made nearly everyone distrust authority figures in government, corporate management, and school, an attitude that naturally carried over into the church. Thus the little church was often embroiled in some kind of controversy.

I was among the first to go to college, our denominational college, not because of slick publicity or generous scholarships, but because my pastor especially urged me to go. Following college, I offered to serve on the staff of a middle-sized church in Flint, Michigan. Single, I worked for a small salary—likely more than I was worth—and rented a room from a kindly widowed grandmother, a member of the congregation.

Now, a mere six years following high school, I found myself in the combined roles of being a new husband, a second-year seminary student, and a first-time pastor. My wife and I worked at denominational headquarters; we lived in a dilapidated house next door to the church, located 17 miles across town from school and jobs.

A bit of a description of the church shows how ordinary our situation was. When we arrived, the church was three years old, grossly underfinanced, and housed in a homemade building with a leaky basement. Cast-off camp meeting benches provided rickety seating. The husband of the Sunday School superintendent was in jail. The church's missionary pledge was paid with money my seminary friends and I received from selling our blood to a medical lab that served area hospitals.

Attendance sometimes reached 75 when most members, a few backsliders, and a visitor or two showed up. The fledgling congregation was a ministry magnet for several genuinely selfless people who wanted a new church in their area of greater Kansas City, a training opportunity for several sacrificial seminary couples, and an ego attraction for strange folks who couldn't make it in other churches.

A volatile Internal Revenue Service midlevel bureaucrat, an average volunteer musician, held our church music hostage with his angry attitudes toward his wife, children, and minister. But he held us as captives because there was no one else to lead the music. And our anguish escalated on those Sundays when our resident musically handicapped guitarist showed up to provide unwelcome backup for the offertory or the soloist.

And the parsonage, an aging 600-square-foot house, was built close to the ground—too close, really. As a result, our furniture fell through to the bare ground when termites infested the wooden floors. To keep warm in winter, the rotting wood around the floor-to-ceiling windows required clear plastic to be stapled to the outside and blankets to be tacked up on the inside. And during warmer months with no air conditioning, the noise from the honky-tonk across the street kept us awake many Saturday nights—inspiring preparation for Sunday's ministry.

Since that first charge, other pastoral assignments presented us with many more challenges. But in every setting, a quiet spiritual development happened inside me; sometimes the process was intentional on my part, and sometimes almost accidental. Though they probably did not realize it, many ordinary people were my tutors.

As I did routine ministry day in and day out, I was enriched while I shared strength of Scripture and tried to love parishioners. I made life-transforming discoveries as I prayed for the people and as they prayed for me. Equally significant, new enrichments stretched and shaped me as I provided pastoral leadership in evangelism, counseling, and discipleship.

The foregoing description of my ministry pilgrimage was included to help us get acquainted. But I intend more—I want us to connect around the common and ordinary so we can see golden opportunities for personal spiritual formation in the routineness of our work. And I want us to cherish possibilities in the now—the present moment—so we do not waste our ministries focused on the past or mesmerized by the future.

HOW PREACHING HELPS ME GROW SPIRITUALLY

A summons from the Lord to preach is an awesome, life-changing experience. Strange as it seems, God chooses to speak through flawed human preachers like us to draw persons to himself. Obviously, effective preaching requires human energy, mental sharpness, and competent communication skills. But it also requires an understanding of Scripture, a willingness to hear from the people, a heart for God in the preacher, and a touch from the Holy One.

In the process of preparing to preach, week by week, it made me a better person and helped me become more useful to God and His church. To borrow T. S. Eliot's terms, it brought me back to the life I had lost in the living. Or to say it more succinctly, it renewed the ministry I sometimes lost in the doing.

Holy Encounter

I experienced amazing spiritual growth when I engaged heart, mind, and will in working to discover the meaning of a passage. Then I had a heart for God and experienced the touch of the Holy One. Being quiet before God many mornings for three or four hours in my study—with an open Bible before me, books around me, and memories of how God had met me so many times in this place—restored my soul and energized my day.

Spiritual formation specialists like Richard Foster would likely classify this shaping of my soul as part of the discipline called study. Foster sees study as a commitment to a process of repetition, concentration, comprehension, and reflection.[3] Additionally for me it also involved a quiet listening and personal application. To borrow Pastor Robert K. Hudnut's term, "It is going to the mat with God."[4]

Encountered preaching means wrestling with the truth of a passage until the preacher knows exactly what it says and then asking the Father to "look me over and see if I am living this truth before I preach it." My mental picture is Jacob wrestling with God and in the process saying, "I will not let you go unless you bless me" (Gen. 32:26).

Such a week-by-week experience of encountering God in Scripture produces a rekindling of the originating vision. That's high-octane spiritual formation for any pastor.

Obsession for Christlikeness

Like believers in every generation for more than 2,000 years, the magnetism of Jesus first attracted me to Him—His life, death, resurrection, mission, and continuing presence. I remember so well the wholehearted "yes" inside me when in my childhood I heard an evangelist call Him "the Magnetic Jesus."

Jesus is the first, last, and everything-in-between inspiration for preaching. In this relationship the Lord opened my eyes to see the differences between the urgent and the important, the passing and the lasting, the peripheral and the essential. This closeness to Jesus gave strength in my inner world so I could face anything. This obsession helped me remember that being, motives, and intentions are more substantive to my work and satisfying to my soul than appearances, images, and impressions.

The more I studied and preached about Christ, the more I wanted to be like Him. Such an obsession must, of course, be rooted in a personal faith, as Brooks explains: "It must be a personal piety, a deep possession in one's own soul of the faith and hope and resolution which he is to offer to fellow human beings for their new life. Nothing but fire kindles fire."[5]

A grand old mentor taught me that hopeful curiosity about Jesus is one big reason people come to hear us preach. The theologian Karl Barth agreed when he wrote, "What the people want to find out and thoroughly understand is, Is it true? . . . They want to find out and thoroughly understand the answer to this one question, and not some answer that beats around the bush."[6]

Somewhere I read about a young beginning pastor who had an excellent education for the ministry. He knew all the academic answers about Jesus, and he knew them well. But as he came to his first Eastertide as a pastor, he couldn't sit still as he prepared his first sermon on the Resurrection. He found himself pacing around the desk saying over and over, "That's the most important truth in all the universe—He's alive. He's alive."

That glorious "ah-ha" moment of meaning happened to me many times—that's spiritual formation at its best.

Accountability to God and People

Since preaching is speaking for God, we must do our best to be sure the message is not confused or garbled—as free as possible from religious goofy dust and phony parroting of the latest theological fad. It is doing our best for the One who loves us most. It is speaking living truth that transforms the listener and the preacher simultaneously as it connects the congregants with the God of the Bible.

C. S. Lewis's great sentence helps us turn accountability from dreary duty into a venture of personal growth: "So many things have now become interesting to me because at first I had to do them whether I like them or not, and thus one is kicked into new countries where one is afterwards at home."[7]

Such accountability makes us better—makes us aware that preaching is a sacred partnership, an adventure of transformation God has shared with us. What an honor and what a trust.

Integrity and Its Satisfactions

It was in what I heard people say about preachers and preaching that I learned the importance of integrity and the inner joy it provides. In preaching, the minister always shows more character than he or she realizes in at least three ways: (1) the preacher must know Christ personally; (2) the preacher must live the message; and (3) the preacher must show from his or her own life a path that others can take. That's an impressive list—both for establishing integrity and receiving its satisfactions.

John R. W. Stott says we are to be visual aids to the people of God.[8] His idea reminds us of two biblical passages. Titus is told, "In everything set them an example by doing what is good. In your teaching show integrity, seriousness and soundness of speech that cannot be condemned, so that those who oppose you may be ashamed because they have nothing bad to say about us" (Titus 2:7-8). And Timothy was instructed to "set an example for the believers in speech, in life, in love, in faith and in purity" (1 Tim. 4:12). Authenticity may not be the only thing that matters in preaching, but nothing else matters much without it.

How Pastoral Care Helped Me Grow Spiritually

Pastoral care at its heart means representing Jesus in the high and low experiences of people's lives. Sometimes called the ministry of presence, it means coming alongside the brokenhearted, ill, afflicted, confused, and dying with the spirit of Jesus. This taking the power of God into one-on-one relations often takes a minister to hospital rooms, jails, emergency rooms, funeral homes, accident sites, angry shouting matches about infidelity, open graves, and sometimes to a family room where the teenager has run away—anywhere human need exists. It signifies experiencing the humility of our own helplessness in the light of the pain and unanswered questions. And it provides us a front seat at seeing how the resources of God make people more than conquerors—to use the apostle Paul's exhilarating phrase.

Every expression of pastoral care possesses astonishing potential for nourishing the minister's interior life. But such a benefit does not happen automatically. Such nourishment only comes when a minister enters every pastoral care contact with a spirit of openness that prays, "God, what do You want to teach me from this ministry opportunity?"

Spiritual Stretch

Pastor David Fisher sets a high standard when he says, "Pastoral work, by its very nature, is a work of grace and therefore must be conducted with all the character and beauty of the grace of God."[9] That insightful sentence is strong enough to make conscientious ministers stretch or quit.

This need for stretching reminds me of a story Bob Benson enjoyed telling. The third grade boy had become the school terror. His behavior was so disruptive the school principal asked the parents to move the boy to a private school. That's exactly what they did. A few days after the move, the parents asked the boy and finally asked his new teacher about his conduct in the new school. The boy gave himself good marks and the new teacher said he was almost a model child in the classroom. At dinner the parents ask the boy about this impressive change. He said, "My new teacher thought I was good, so I was." That modern parable can be applied to the details of ministry in our time.

While serving in Colorado Springs, one of the mature aging nuns at St. Frances Hospital asked if I knew a certain doctor. I agreed that I knew him well and I was happy to report that he was a serious Christian, though not a member of the congregation I served. She told me, "We nuns believe Dr. D. is more like Jesus than any physician we have ever seen."

I joked with her and asked, "Can you say that about any pastor who calls in this hospital?"

She smiled sweetly and didn't reply. I think that was a nonverbal answer that meant some pastors, including me, needed to do a little better. But that day I heard her strongly imply that the spirit of Jesus is important in lots of relationships—even casual, chance meetings in businesses, schools, and airports.

The idea stretches me—I want to be more like Christ. My pastoral contacts make it possible for me to show His Spirit in many different relationships.

Love Matters

Like too many pastors before and after me, I started out in ministry assuming a solid education, skills, degrees, and competency were the roots of effective ministry. But I was short on expressing agape and affection. The people of God, however, soon taught me that the first step to becoming an effective pastor is to love the people, warts and all. And the second step, or perhaps the other side of the first step, is to give them the opportunity to love me. The more love, the fewer squabbles and controversies. The more love, the more pastor and people trust each other.

The apostle Paul understood this two-way love affair between pastor and people when he wrote, "Watch what God does, and then you do it, like children who learn proper behavior from their parents. Mostly what God does is love you. Keep company with him and learn a life of love. Observe how Christ loved us. His love was not cautious but extravagant. He didn't love in order to get something from us but to give everything of himself to us. Love like that" (Eph. 5:1-2, TM).

Living Examples of Faith

In pastoral care you get to see how faith works in tough times—that builds your own faith.

Pansy Reynolds was well into her 80s when I became her pastor. One Sunday after I preached on the strength of Christ, she stood and asked if she could say a few words. My first thought was this is an unnecessary interruption, but I was wrong. She gave this witness: "I have lived long enough to bury three adult children. My heart is broken, but the power of my faith sustains me. And it was the care of the people of God that helped me cope." That day she connected pastoral care and preaching in the eyes of the entire congregation, but she helped me much more personally in the strengthening of my faith.

Dependence and Unique Partnership

While going to the needy person is the usual way pastoral care is provided, it is the minister's inner spiritual strengths that authenticate the going and make the contact significantly different from a visit from the next-door neighbor or even the hospital call of the physician. The pastor's visit is unique because the minister represents the Lord and the combined fellowship of the local church, and some believe the contemporary pastor represents the church of all generations wherever it may be found. The difference shows in our attitude, our conversation, and our sense of expectancy of what the Lord will do in this meeting.

Our pattern is Jesus and the incarnational way He related to people.

After discussing how his conscience never has Alzheimer's when it came to missing a pastoral call, Pastor David Hensen describes the miracle of presence that takes place when the pastor goes to the needy person: "When I arrive in the room of suffering, love takes over. My heart beats faster, my consciousness sharpens, and my innards feel less stable. Compassion happens. What began onerously ends sympathetically. Human kindness ignited by a Spirit spark leads to a Spirit prayer for healing. What a strange turn of events! I walked into a hospital room grumpy because I'm missing the fourth quarter of a football game, and I walk out feeling like Mother Teresa, Jr. *It rarely fails.*"[10]

Agape Bonds Forged in Crises

A holy bond often develops between persons suffering deep crises and a pastor who represents the Lord to them in their dark days. This is the reality that often makes a family in the church imply or even say to a new pastor, "Our previous minister, Pastor Jones, was the best pastor this church ever had—we'll always believe that!"

Sadly, the new pastor wonders why this family can't get over their affection for the former pastor. It is the "fellowship of suffering" or going through "the valley of the shadow of death" together that creates this bond. Across the years of my ministry, I can remember at least 20 or 25 relationships of loss and suffering that connected me with people as if we were kin. It is not what I did that made the bond; it was what we suffered together. Most of these relationships should be affirmed and appreciated by the new pastor because they are living trophies of the spirit of Jesus at work.

HOW OTHER EXPRESSIONS OF MINISTRY
HELPED ME GROW SPIRITUALLY

Other functions of ministry have a way of shaping our spiritual well-being. I found that especially true in evangelism and worship.

Evangelism

Evangelism, the heartbeat of the gospel, is the passionate concern given us by Jesus that all human beings need the Savior to forgive their sins and enable them to live a quality life now and forever. Few pastors serve in ministry very long before they realize a church cannot be healthy if it does not have a constant flow of new converts, and new converts need to be discipled. But the two sides of the Great Commission—win and teach—are easy to neglect if not programmed into the schedule like worship, Sunday School, and administrative meetings.

The list of personal spiritual formation possibilities in evangelism are long, but let me list three highlights.

- **Exercise builds spiritual stamina.** Like exercise for my body, my spiritual well-being requires that I be involved in faith sharing on a one-on-one basis with specific individuals.
- **Teaching reinforces learning.** Helping individuals learn and practice the spiritual disciplines—the teach side of the Great Commission—provides a personal refresher course for the pastor.
- **Significance of transformation.** Seeing lives transformed and living long enough to see the faith I shared with individuals carried over into the next generation is a significant fulfillment of my own spiritual formation.

Worship

What a celebration of grace and gratitude when God's people come together to sing, read Scripture, pray, praise, and hear the Word of God proclaimed. One thoughtful writer said that for worship to have maximum impact it needs three parts: (1) celebration, (2) reflection, and (3) application.

Or think of it this way: a pastor has the privilege of leading worshipers into the presence of God—something bigger, nobler, and more momentous than taking them into the combined presence of prime ministers, presidents, and kings and queens of all ages. There is a holy something that takes place in the family of God when the pastor prays for the people and shares a message God has customized for this congregation.

When authentic worship takes place, there is a sense of awe and adventure—awe at the place of worship, and adventure as the worshipers take the challenges, commandments, commitments, and covenants into the world where they work and live.

The personal spiritual formation lessons I learned while leading worship are many, but let me list a few.

- **Self-examination.** Standing in such a holy place calls for frequent self-examination and for a humble admission of divine enablement.

- **Clarified perspective.** Leading worship clarifies my perspective about lesser issues in the church and in my life as well.
- **God-focused.** Worship preferences of pastor and congregation are not as important as what Jesus told the woman at the well: "A time is coming and has now come when the true worshipers will worship the Father in spirit and truth, for they are the kind of worshipers the Father seeks. God is spirit, and his worshipers must worship in spirit and in truth" (John 4:23-24). That phrase, "the kind of worshipers the Father seeks," is an enlightening concept that changes worship from self-focus to God-focus—what it is He wants.

SPIRITUAL FORMATION LESSONS ORDINARY PEOPLE TAUGHT ME

Faithful Christians in every congregation I served impacted my spiritual development. The following are only random choices of hundreds of examples of people who contributed to my spiritual development.

"Pastor—You Need the Grace of Receiving"

WS taught me this hard lesson. After I served her during the unexpected death of her husband, she started bringing wonderful, expensive toys to my preschool-age children. Her generosity became embarrassing to me, so I reminded her that what I did for her was done in Jesus' name, with no thought or need of a reward. Then I clumsily asked her not to bring more gifts. In a quiet voice she replied, "Pastor, you have the gift of giving, but you need to develop the gift of receiving." I did need to develop that gift, and I have improved.

"Pastor—Your Perspective Is Simply Nonsense"

CH made me eager to reverse my policy of having no contact with the churches I previously served. I announced at the time of my resignation that when we left, there would be no contact, no letters, no phone calls. She thought my position silly, so she waited until our son was born in the year after we left that church. She wrote him his first letter when he was just two or three months old and said, "Your dad told us we couldn't write him, but he didn't say not to write you. Could you tell me how your parents are doing?"

"Pastor—There Is a Time When Prayer Is All We Have"

EH taught me the power of intercession, Bible reading, and faith. She and her husband were good common people—he a retired factory worker and she a housewife and mother. Bud had emphysema so bad that he had to fight for every breath, and nights were always the worst. I often called on them on my way home, about 9:00 or 10:00 at night, after a committee meeting or a church service. The idea was to pray for God's help for them to get through the night. Often after I left, she read Scripture aloud for an hour or two while her husband fought for every breath. Her prayers, perseverance, and Scripture reading kept him alive for months.

"Pastor—Did You Know This About Yourself?"

Three men about my age in one church I served were fatally ill but couldn't die. Their suffering went on for months, and I tried to be a good pastor to them. Most of the time I was in their homes several times each week. But I found it harder and harder to call, and I couldn't figure out why. Then it dawned on me that I was struggling with my own mortality. That experience sent me back to the Scriptures to see what they say. And I discovered in a new way what the Bible means when Jesus said, "I am the resurrection and the life. He who believes in me will live, even though he dies" (John 11:25).

"Pastor—We're Family, Not Business Associates"

Call him Joe. He was a member of the official decision group in the church, and he was pleased to frustrate pastors by being against everything and for nothing. One night I took what I thought was strong leadership and let him know in no uncertain terms what I thought of his tactics. I felt satisfyingly smug about my reaction. But about 1:30 the next morning he had a serious heart attack and I was called to pray with him in the emergency room. All the way to the hospital God worked on me. From then until now I have been careful to keep short accounts with those who disagree with me. The lesson—I was Joe's pastor more than the head of the corporation called the church.

"Pastor—God Isn't Always Predictable"

Let me tell you about a collision of memory, mystery, and miracle. The phone rang in the little office/study in the church located in a northwestern town. It was about 10:00 in the morning, and the call was from three aging children in their middle 50s and early 60s. Their dad, well along in his 80s, was dying and in a coma. Years previously he had been a faithful Christian, but someone did him wrong at church. He walked out, never returned, and turned to a shoddy life of drinking and womanizing. From that moment of leaving, he never mentioned Christ in the hearing of his children again across all those years. But they had a faint memory of how it used to be so long ago, so they wanted this preacher whose name they found in the phone book to do something spiritual for their dad.

Out of a sense of obligation I visited the old man with his children gathered around his bed in a rest home. The scene was bleak—an inexperienced young preacher, the children old enough to be the pastor's parents, and their dying father in a coma. My attitude was bad, and my body language clearly communicated, "How could you expect me or God to do anything now?"

I did my duty. I read scripture, prayed, and left. No response from the patient. But about an hour later, he had a few moments of lucidity and said, "Tell the preacher I take Jesus." And he was gone.

Imagine my surprise. That day I learned that mystery, miracle, and memory can teach us a lot about God. That day I learned God has no hopeless cases. That lesson still informs my own spiritual development. And the promise is true, "God is able to do exceedingly more than we are able to ask or think."

WHAT SPIRITUAL FORMATION OPPORTUNITIES DOES GOD HAVE PLANNED FOR US TODAY?

Why not wring every shred of boredom or negativity out of thoughts about words such as "routine," "common," and "daily"? Why not cherish what one writer called blessed ordinariness? The challenge is to use the sacred potential of day-by-day expressions of ministry for our own spiritual development. Then our homesickness for God—this yearning to know Him better—will not have to be put on hold until we are able to visit some distant shrine or some favorite mentor.

Let's salute these words—"routine," "common," and "daily"—as describing a holy adventure and a special place of meeting with God.

The majesty and practicality of using close-by expressions of ministry are poetically captured by essayist Wendell Berry: "The world cannot be discovered by a journey of miles, no matter how long, but only by a spiritual journey, a journey of one inch, very arduous and humbling and joyful, by which we arrive at the ground at our feet, and learn to be at home."[11]

That one-inch journey can begin and continue by making the apostle Paul's testimony our own: "By no means do I count myself an expert in all of this, but I've got my eye on the goal, where God is beckoning us onward—to Jesus. I'm off and running, and I'm not turning back" (Phil. 3:13-14, TM). Then next Sunday's sermon, long before it is preached, becomes a moving message from God to us. The healing word offered the sick, hope shared with the dying, and comfort given to the grieving become a part of our spiritual development. Writings concerning the inner life often include the big 10 disciplines: prayer, Scripture, centering on Christ, friendship, service, study, listening, simplicity, charity, and humility. Abundant opportunities to practice every discipline on this list and more are available in every pastorate nearly every day.

Go for it!

Notes

1. *Lectures on Preaching* (Grand Rapids: Baker Book House, 1969), 70.

2. *Barlett's Familar Quotations* (Boston: Little and Brown, 1980), 523.

3. Richard Foster, *Celebration of Discipline* (New York: Harper and Row, 1978), 58-60.

4. Robert K. Hudnut, *This People, This Parish* (Grand Rapids: Zondervan, 1986), 96.

5. Batsell Barrett Baxter, *The Heart of the Yale Lectures* (New York: Macmillan Company, 1947), 32.

6. As quoted by Frederick Buechner, *The Eyes of the Heart* (San Francisco: HarperSanFrancisco, 1999), 74.

7. *Quotable Lewis*, Wayne Martindale and Jerry Root, eds. (Wheaton, Ill.: Tyndale House Publishers, 1989), 170.

8. John R. W. Stott, *Between Two Worlds* (Grand Rapids: Eerdmans, 1982), 78.

9. David Fisher, *The 21st Century Pastor* (Grand Rapids: Zondervan, 1996), 146.

10. David Hansen, *The Power of Loving Your Church* (Minneapolis: Bethany, 1998), 68-69.

11. As quoted by Sarah York, *Pilgrim Heart* (San Francisco: Jossey-Bass, 2001), ix.

Douglas S. Hardy grew up in New Brunswick, Canada, where he received spiritual guidance from several adults in his home church before leaving for studies at Eastern Nazarene College (B.A.), Northeastern University (M.Ed.), Fuller Theological Seminary (M.A.), and Boston University (Ph.D.). His doctoral degree from Boston University in psychology of religion focused on the interface between Christian spiritual direction practice and psychoanalytic object relations theory. He has been the recipient of formal spiritual direction from 10 different directors over a span of 22 years and has served as a spiritual director to others for 11 years. An ordained elder in the Church of the Nazarene, Doug's fundamental pastoral calling is to come alongside others to help facilitate their alignment with God. He has done this in parish pastoral ministry for 7 years in California, as a professor of psychology in a Christian liberal arts college for 13 years, and now as professor of spiritual formation at Nazarene Theological Seminary in Kansas City. He has published articles and reviews in *CrossCurrents,* the *International Journal for the Psychology of Religion,* the *Journal of Psychology and Christianity,* the *Journal of Psychology and Theology,* and contributed a chapter to the book *Spiritual Formation, Counseling, and Psychotherapy* (Nova Science Publishers, 2003). Doug is blessed to be married to Anne and to coparent their three children, Alexander, Lia, and Elena.

9

The Pastor and Spiritual Direction

Douglas S. Hardy

🌿 WHEN CHARLES ASHWORTH, THE RECENTLY WIDOWED, MIDDLE-aged priest in the novel *Glittering Images*,[1] becomes so obsessed with the faults of others that he can't see his own weaknesses, he yields to sexual temptation, compromises his ordination vows, and then collapses emotionally. His restoration is facilitated, not as we might expect, by the clinical expertise of a doctor, a psychotherapist, or a social worker, but by a priest-turned-monk who functions as Ashworth's spiritual director.

Providing those who are called to a specifically religious vocation with access to a spiritual director is a long-standing tradition within Anglican, Roman Catholic, and Orthodox branches of the Christian Church. Consequently, it is not unusual for clergy in these traditions to meet with such a person for spiritual resourcing and renewal. Protestant pastors, especially in Evangelical denominations less familiar with this history, may have no experience with this practice. I was fortunate to be introduced to spiritual direction as a resource for ministers at the Evangelical seminary I attended some 20 years ago. The school had just established a collaborative relationship with a Benedictine monastery and instituted its first ever program in spiritual formation for seminarians, including a spiritual direction component. What was groundbreaking then is almost commonplace now. We live in a time when information about and opportunity to receive spiritual direction are dramatically increasing, and perhaps none too soon.[2] More than just another fad or trend, it is a sign that an important need in the life of the Church has been recognized and is beginning to be addressed.

WHAT NEED DOES SPIRITUAL DIRECTION ADDRESS?

In the spirit of John Wesley, who functioned as a spiritual director to many and who insisted that the Christian faith can only be authentically lived in the context of disciplined accountability,[3] I begin with the claim that all Christians, especially pastors, need spiritual guidance or direction. Why?

111

- We have an unsatisfied yearning for God that often goes unheeded. We need others to help affirm the value of seeking God.
- We both seek God *and* resist God; we want closeness to God *and* space from God; we want to be challenged *and* to be safe. We need others to help us recognize the ways we create distance between God and ourselves.
- Spiritual growth doesn't happen naturally; it requires response and intention. Taking the process for granted is dangerous to the soul. Spiritual direction helps us with intentionality.
- Aspects of the spiritual life, such as praying or almsgiving, are difficult. We need encouragement and practical help from those who are wise from experience.
- We are prone to distort the spiritual life into something it is not meant to be, such as legalism or the pursuit of pleasure. Directors help us recognize and correct these distortions.
- The "way forward" spiritually is unique for each individual; diverse journeys require careful attending to each individual's experience of God. Directors help us practice discernment and avoid unhealthy conformity.

Although Rev. Ashworth in *Glittering Images* is a fictional character living in 1930s England, his personal and professional disintegration described in the novel is frighteningly realistic and his challenges not unlike those faced by Christian ministers at the beginning of the 21st century. Like him, a pastor today may say to others "I'm fine, everything's fine"[4] when, in reality, his or her spiritual state may be quite weak. Because "High and wide is the gate which leads to self-deception and illusion,"[5] ministers are often unaware of the ways in which their personal and professional lives may diverge from the gospel they believe in and preach to others. And because Christian ministers have so much at stake regarding their public reputation, they often tend to shield themselves from the awareness that evil has a pull on their lives, rather than open up to the healing, sanctifying, and equipping grace of the Holy Spirit.

Yes, Christian pastors need assistance from others to remain authentic disciples of Jesus Christ. Ironically, though passionately advocating for Christian community among their parishioners, they often find themselves alone and isolated. As a pastor or pastor-to-be, you will soon discover, if you haven't already, that no matter how talented and "successful" you are as a Christian minister, you are "quite unable to heal [your]self."[6] You need others to companion you on the way. Yet with whom can you honestly share the deepest questions and concerns of your heart?

The purpose of this chapter is twofold: First, I want to introduce you to Christian spiritual direction, a form of companioning that, by definition, centers on the heart of the matter—your relationship with God in Christ. If received regularly and reverently, this companioning can function as a valuable means of grace for your ongoing personal and ministerial formation. Second, I want to invite you to prayerfully consider seeking such spiritual companionship for yourself. To do this you will need to make an informed assessment, so let us begin with a definition and description.

WHAT *IS* SPIRITUAL DIRECTION? (AND WHAT IS IT *NOT?*)

Each of the commonly known world religions—Judaism, Hinduism, Islam, Buddhism, and Christianity—has a tradition of offering spiritual direction. For Christians it is but one of several methods for providing believers with "soul care." As the name suggests, it has to do with tuning in to the spiritual dimension of a person's life, that is, a person's encounter with and response to the Holy Spirit of God, *and* with offering direction or guidance to that person in the process. Understood broadly, this guidance can come through a variety of people, such as parents, friends, teachers, and authors, and through a variety of ministries of the church, such as worship, preaching, and education. It is often informally given and unconsciously received. In moments of crisis or periods of special need it may be more formally sought and consciously received. However, for Christians who are serious about a lifelong process of deepening their spiritual lives and integrating that depth with a maturity of body, mind, and emotions, spiritual direction in a more regular and consistent form is needed. This is certainly the case for pastors.

In this more technical meaning then, spiritual direction is the facilitation of one's spiritual formation in a covenanted relationship with either another individual or a small group,[7] formalized in regular meetings for inquiry, conversation, and reflection around one's personal experience. Here the designated spiritual *director* is one who, by virtue of personal holiness, spiritual maturity, and the gifts and graces for counseling, helps the *directee* (the one receiving spiritual direction) to discern and pay attention to the presence and work of God in his or her life. The designated directee is one who, aware of a deep spiritual hunger, makes himself or herself available to a director for focused examination of that hunger and shared listening to God. In short, spiritual direction is "help given by one Christian to another that enables that person to pay attention to God's personal communication to him or her, to respond to this personally communicating God, to grow in intimacy with this God, and to live out the consequence of the relationship."[8] The person who would serve as such a guide or director needs to have "some capacity to be helpful to the other by virtue of personal graced experience, the gift of discernment, experience with self and others, and sufficient knowledge of the spiritual tradition and ordinary human development."[9]

Some fundamental assumptions undergird this intentional practice of spiritual direction:

- The Holy Spirit is the ultimate director (Rom. 8:14-16). Thus, the "directing" by the director is pointing to the person and work of the Spirit, modeling sensitivity and encouraging responsiveness to that Spirit.
- The practice is relational. The relationship between director and directee serves to nurture a healthy relationship between the directee and God and between the directee and his or her significant others.
- A commonality of faith and mutuality of experience with God exists between director and directee. Even though there is a distinction in roles that keeps the focus primarily on the faith experience of the directee, both are pilgrims on the journey and, thus, bound together ultimately as brothers and sisters in Christ.
- The director respects the individuality, freedom, and responsibility of the directee. The director serves the directee through respectful listening, gentle probing, and, on occasion, firm challenging, but never assumes an authoritarian stance or attempts to do for the directee what the directee must do for himself or herself.

These descriptions and definitions may seem similar to other practices of soul care with which you are already familiar, for example, discipling, pastoral counseling, and psychotherapy. There are important differences, however. "Discipling" is a term that is often used to describe intense spiritual-mentoring relationships that help the church accomplish its educational and reproductive missions. The most recent discipling movement to emerge in North America has been largely Evangelical and Reformed (and sometimes fundamentalist) in its theological orientation, didactic in methodology, and hierarchical in its relational structure.[10] While Christian spiritual direction is clearly about making disciples of Jesus Christ, it is not primarily about teaching the Bible or doctrine through content acquisition and mastery. Discipleship programs, though serving important educational objectives, are usually too packaged to allow for individualized spiritual direction. Further, unlike the discipler who meets the disciple as an authority with an agenda to be covered, the spiritual director typically does not bring an agenda to the directee other than that of listening for God and working with what emerges out of the process of a particular meeting.

Psychotherapy is a secular form of soul care grounded in the social and behavioral sciences. Pastoral counseling is a 20th-century development out of mainline Protestantism that seeks to make secular counseling resources available in a pastoral (and explicitly theological) setting. Both share spiritual direction's commitment to skilled listening, contracted meetings, and concern for the well-being of the directee. Pastoral counseling, like spiritual

direction, uses God language and works within the faith context of the
counselee. Many psychotherapists, not only those whose personal faith commitment is Christian, are sensitive to the spiritual concerns of their clients.
Consequently, the lines that divide these practices are not as sharp as some
have drawn them and there is significant potential for cooperative and inte-
grative work at the boundaries. Nonetheless, each practice tends to focus on
a different agenda and reflect a different goal. Psychotherapy is concerned
with the healing of bio-psycho-socio wounds, especially those typically
known as psychological disorders and categorized in the latest version of the
DSM.[11] It may involve the use of psychotropic drugs, exploration of unre-
solved past conflicts, and/or adjustments in cognitive and behavioral patterns. Pastoral counseling is concerned with helping otherwise healthily
functioning individuals identify, strategize, and solve problems in the daily
living environments of family, work, community, and religion/spirituality.
The counseling is often solicited in a time of crisis and tends to be short-
term until the person is sufficiently resourced to address the problem.

Spiritual direction, like psychotherapy, is concerned with personal
healing and wholeness and, like pastoral counseling, is concerned with the
problems and challenges of everyday living. But the spiritual director is *not*
primarily a healer or a problem solver. Rather, he or she will help the directee discover, attend to, and respond to the divine presence in the midst
of the realities of past, present, and future living. These differences can be
summarized as follows:

	Goal of the Soulcare	**Role of the Caregiver**
Discipling	Passing on the core content and practices of the faith	Tutor
Psychotherapy	Healing the bio-psycho-socio wounds of psychological disorders	Healer
Pastoral Counseling	Identifying, strategizing, and solving life problems within a faith context	Advocate
Spiritual Direction	Discovering, attending, and responding to the presence of God	Guide

Because spiritual direction functions integratively by placing all of life within a spiritual perspective, it is important that pastors-as-directees avail themselves of whatever resources will assist growth toward maturity, whether discipling, pastoral counseling, psychotherapy, or some other helpful practice. Though each is unique, they can be complementary. I have been fortunate in my Christian walk—including my years as a pastor and theological educator—to be the recipient at various times of discipling programs *and* counseling *and* therapy *and* spiritual direction. Let me share with you some of my experience with one-to-one spiritual direction as a way of helping you know what typically happens in a meeting between a spiritual director and directee.

WHAT CAN I EXPECT OF A SPIRITUAL DIRECTION SESSION?

The first sessions of a spiritual direction relationship are usually exploratory. The focus is on getting to know each other, beginning to name the agenda of the directee, and discerning the degree to which the potential director is a good match for the directee's needs. My very first spiritual director asked me to write a "spiritual autobiography" for him to read and then for us to discuss. The conversations that sprang from this document not only helped him to better understand my spiritual journey but also helped both of us to see more clearly what I was expecting from spiritual direction. Further, these talks provided me with an opportunity to see how it felt to be listened to by this person.

If, after the first few meetings, the director and directee agree that they are a good match for a spiritual direction relationship, they usually covenant to meet together regularly based on a shared understanding of

- the nature and purpose of spiritual direction
- the particular concerns and needs of the directee at this point in his or her life
- the particular gifts and graces that this director will bring to the relationship at this point in his or her life
- the frequency and length of meetings
- the form and amount of remuneration for the director, if any
- a method and timing for periodic evaluation of the direction relationship

Most directors prefer to meet with directees on a once-a-month schedule for one-to-one direction, although meetings may be more frequent in the early stages of the relationship, during retreats, or in times of crisis. When spiritual direction is given and received in a small-group setting, meetings are typically held once a week or biweekly, in order to give adequate time to attend to all group members. Sometimes spiritual direction can be offered by phone, letter, or e-mail, although face-to-face meetings are preferable whenever possible. Many persons who make themselves available for the ministry of spiritual direction do so without expectation of remuneration. Some are laypersons for whom this is a gift they exercise as their volunteer ministry to the church. Some are religious professionals who are salaried and who do spiritual direction "on the side." There are those, however, who as professionally trained and "full time" spiritual directors depend on their directees for income to make a living, much like pastors depend on their parishioners for their income. These directors will negotiate a fee with their directees, often on a sliding scale that respects the financial resources of the directee.

Once a director and directee agree on how to proceed, their ongoing meetings will take on the uniqueness one might expect from the artful dance that "comes in meshing the sensitivities of the director with the contours of the person seeking direction."[12] Spiritual directors have differing personalities, differing gifts, differing training, and differing theological/ecclesial traditions within which they anchor their work. My own spiritual directors have been Roman Catholic and Presbyterian, male and female, introvert and extrovert, clergy and lay. Each brought unique gifts and graces to the table, each had a distinct approach to the work of spiritual direction, and yet there are important commonalities that clearly mark their work *as* spiritual direction. Over the years of their wonderfully diverse ministry to me, I have come to expect the following from *anyone* who would serve as my spiritual director:

- Welcome me with a spirit of hospitality; the director will communicate to me verbally and nonverbally that he or she deeply cares for me.
- Invite me to describe the specific, concrete features of my daily experience, whether dramatic or mundane, uplifting or depressing, joyful or painful.
- Through conversation (interspersed liberally with periods of silence and prayer), help me pay attention to my experience and discern God's presence and activity there, often through asking me basic questions, such as, "Where is God in all this?" or "What might God be inviting you to notice?" or "What is it like for you when you pray?"
- Assist me in discerning the meaning and significance of my faith life, and encourage me to make choices in line with those discernments.
- Nurture me in my relationship with God and with significant others in my life.
- Suggest exercises, activities, or disciplines to help me continue to

attend to and respond positively to God in between direction sessions; these "homework" assignments are offered with freedom to experiment and learn by trial-and-error.

- Hold me accountable to God through gentle, yet firm inquiry.
- Affirm me as a child of God and encourage me with the hope of one who trusts in the Spirit of God to transform people into the image of Jesus Christ.

Clearly, not just anyone *can* or *will* serve as my spiritual director. Since my first spiritual direction relationship many years ago, I have had to seek out a new director nine times—mostly because either I or my spiritual director moved to a location too far away to continue meeting. Each transition has forced me to revisit a sometimes daunting challenge—grieving the loss of a special companion and then finding someone new who *could* and *would* be my spiritual director.

How Do I Find a Spiritual Director?

The first step in finding a spiritual director is to make it a matter of prayer. Spiritual direction is the Holy Spirit's business, and what better way to prepare for paying attention to the Spirit *in* a direction session than to learn to pay attention to the Spirit *during* the process of arranging for that first session. If God has awakened in your heart a desire to deepen your faith life, you can be confident that God cares about you and will see to it that you find those who can help resource you (Luke 11:9-13). Prayer, then, becomes the process whereby you deepen your trust in God, clarify your desires, and hone your readiness to listen. Praying will help you know what qualities you need to look for in a director and will prompt you to notice these qualities in those around you, even as you ask God, "Who is it that I should ask to be my director?" Directors are people who pray and, therefore, they will be tuning in to that same Spirit as they ask God the mirror question to yours: "Who is it that I should make myself available to?" A rich biblical example of this spiritual dynamic is found in Luke 1 where a pregnant and seeking Mary encounters a pregnant and receptive Elizabeth. Each was responsive to a birthing process instigated by the Holy Spirit; each needed the other to find encouragement and guidance for an awesome responsibility. It is no surprise that Mary stayed with Elizabeth for three months. She had found her spiritual director.

With prayer as the underpinning, there are a number of initiatives you can take to locate and explore possibilities with potential directors:

- Begin by assessing your most immediate circle of relationships; is there someone you already know who might be prepared and ready to serve as your director?

- Consider those persons you already view as spiritual leaders (not necessarily the same thing as ecclesiastical leaders), whom you respect for their life of prayer and devotion to God.
- Check your denominational programming for resources in spiritual development that may include referrals to spiritual directors.
- Call or visit local retreat centers where the tradition of Christian spiritual direction is understood and directors often have established practices.
- Consult with national organizations that train and network spiritual directors; they often publish directories.[13]

If you have more than one potential spiritual director, there are a number of variables that may be important to you in making a choice: you may prefer a male director or a female director, one who is younger or one who is older, a director who is single or one who is married, a fellow pastor or a layperson, someone within your denomination or completely outside it, someone like you in personality or someone very different from you. These preferences reflect your need to find someone with whom you can feel safe, whom you can trust to hold in confidence what you reveal, and whose other positions or roles do not create a potential conflict of interest. It is entirely appropriate to be sensitive to these preferences and work within them, as long as you don't allow spiritual direction to become a protective shell dedicated to preserving the status quo. The history of Christianity is replete with evidence that God works effectively through *all* kinds of people, and it just may be that the spiritual director who could be of most help to you is surprisingly different from what you would imagine.

After a recent move, I entered into the familiar but still challenging process of looking for a new spiritual director. Through the recommendation of a friend, I contacted a religious leader in town who was experienced as a director and willing to meet with me. He seemed like an ideal director for my new situation, and so we began meeting regularly. In spite of his care for me, I began to feel uncomfortable in our sessions and troubled in my spirit in between meetings as I wrestled with his guidance. Although I had some hunches as to what might be at issue, I never had the opportunity to find out, for barely four months into our relationship I received word that he had been convicted of wrongdoing in his parish, relieved of his ministerial credentials, and relocated to another community. What an unexpected turn of events! What a vulnerable and unsettled feeling for me as a directee! I had prayed for God's leading in finding a director, believed that this director was an answer to that prayer, and then it all fell apart leaving me back at square one. Spiritual direction—a practice I strongly believe in and support—is risky. So much is at stake. This is why ongoing prayer is so critical. You see, praying through this disappointing and painful experience helped me to see I was really *not* back at square one. Though a little shell-shocked, I had a deeper understanding of what I needed in spiritual direction and the kind of person who could best help me. So now my current director—a wonderful Benedictine sister—is clearly God's healing presence to me in ways that I could not have imagined before the false start.

Directors and directees are imperfect human beings, yet human beings in whose weakness God's strength can be revealed (2 Cor. 12:9-10). In looking for a spiritual director, then, be careful to not be misled by external appearances. Instead, look for the fruit that indicates that this person is truly a good director:

- Anchored in God and practicing spiritual disciplines
- A *receiver* of spiritual direction
- Willing and able to companion you in the joys and struggles of life
- Dedicated to directing you to God and helping you discover His divine presence
- Distanced enough from the contemporary culture of control and compulsive activity to help create space to encounter the Spirit of God

Whether for one meeting only or for a sustained relationship over many years, finding a spiritual director is well worth the effort if you want this form of spiritual guidance.

HOW DO I KNOW IF I NEED A SPIRITUAL DIRECTOR?

Imagine it is Sunday night, the end of a busy Lord's day. Your pastoral role and duties concluded for another week, you arrive home and sit down to unwind. Perhaps it was a good day; perhaps it was a difficult day. Knowing that Monday is but several hours away, you wonder if this is all there is. A measure of dissatisfaction tugs at your soul, but you are not sure what to do about it or who to talk to. Might your heart be communicating a need for spiritual direction?

I have already made the claim that all of us need spiritual guidance or direction, and this is especially true for a pastor or a pastor-in-training. In the reading of this chapter you have been introduced to a tradition of spiritual companioning wherein spiritual direction is given in an intentional, regular, and covenanted form either one-to-one or in a small group. Now I want to invite you to prayerfully consider whether this is a time for you to seek a spiritual director and commit to the practice of meeting regularly as a constituent part of your ongoing personal and ministerial formation.

Here are some signs that may indicate your need for and readiness to enter into a spiritual direction relationship:

- You long for a deeper relationship with God.

- You are restless for something "more" in life but are not sure what it is.
- You feel stale spiritually.
- You are subject to significant and regular temptation to sin.
- You struggle with existential questions about God or the Church.
- Your understanding of God and faith is changing, and you feel disoriented.
- You are uncertain about your calling, your identity, your purpose in life.
- You are experiencing loss or grief.
- You lack in spiritual discipline.
- You need to grow in prayer but don't know how.
- You need to make an important decision and want help with discernment.
- You want a spiritual companion for the journey.
- You need someone to listen to you.

Do *you* need someone to be a "holy listener" in your life right now? Then heed the advice of John Wesley and "ask counsel of [one] that watcheth over thy soul."[14] Whatever the prompt, whether the urgency of a crisis or simply a desire to know God better in the midst of the very ordinary, take seriously the call to be spiritually directed by others. It is a vital part of your call to ministry.

Notes

1. The first in a series of Anglican clergy novels by author Susan Howatch. The series, published in paperback form by Fawcett Crest, New York, reintroduces contemporary readers to the long-standing but much-neglected tradition of Christian spiritual direction. They are, in order of publication: *Glittering Images* (1987), *Glamorous Powers* (1988), *Ultimate Prizes* (1989), *Scandalous Risks* (1990), *Mystical Paths* (1992), *and Absolute Truths* (1994). The second novel, *Glamorous Powers*, includes the most in-depth description of a spiritual direction relationship.

2. Christian and theological bookstores have shelves devoted to an ever-expanding literature on the topic, seminaries and specialized training institutes are offering courses and certificates to prepare professionals, and a growing number of networks of spiritual directors are forming around professional concerns such as continuing education, supervision, credentialing, and publishing. The web site of the organization Spiritual Directors International is representative of these developments: http://www.sdi world.org.

3. See W. Paul Jones, "Communal Spiritual Direction: The Wesleyan Movement as Model," chapter 3 in *The Art of Spiritual Direction: Giving and Receiving Spiritual Guidance* (Nashville: Upper Room, 2002), 65-96; and Wesley D. Tracy, "Spiritual Direction in the Wesleyan-Holiness Tradition," chapter 6 in Gary W. Moon and David G.

Benner, eds., *Spiritual Direction and the Care of Souls: A Guide to Christian Approaches and Practices* (Downers Grove, Ill.: InterVarsity, 2004), 115-51.

4. Quoted by Charles Ashworth in Susan Howatch, *Glittering Images*, 133.

5. Quoted by Ashworth's spiritual director, Jonathan Darrow, ibid., 176.

6. An admission of Jonathan Darrow about his need for a spiritual director, even though he was a spiritual director to many, Susan Howatch, *Glamorous Powers*, 353.

7. For the purposes of this chapter—a brief introduction to spiritual direction—I will focus almost exclusively on the more normative one-to-one, individual form of the practice. I want the reader, however, to be aware of the growing interest in small-group spiritual direction and to consider it as a viable option. For descriptions of how group spiritual direction operates, see Jeanette Bakke, "Group Spiritual Direction," chapter in *Holy Invitations: Exploring Spiritual Direction* (Grand Rapids: Baker, 2000); Rose Mary Doughety, *Group Spiritual Direction: Community for Discernment* (New York: Paulist, 1995); and W. Paul Jones, "Communal Spiritual Direction: The Wesleyan Movement as Model," chapter 3 in *The Art of Spiritual Direction: Giving and Receiving Spiritual Guidance* (Nashville: Upper Room, 2002), 65-96.

8. William Barry and William Connolly, *The Practice of Spiritual Direction* (San Francisco: Harper and Row, 1982), 8.

9. Janet Ruffing, *Uncovering Stories of Faith* (New York: Paulist, 1989), 18.

10. The parachurch organization Navigators is illustrative of this approach.

11. *The Diagnostic and Statistical Manual of Mental Disorders*, published by the American Psychiatric Association. The most current version as of this writing is the *DSM IV-TR* (2000).

12. Jones, *The Art of Spiritual Direction*, 39.

13. Visit http://www.sdiworld.org/html/train.html for a listing of retreat centers and training programs for spiritual directors.

14. John Wesley, "Upon Our Lord's Sermon on the Mount, Discourse the Third" in Albert C. Outler, ed., *The Works of John Wesley*, Vol. 1 (Nashville: Abingdon, 1984), 512.

For Further Reading

Bakke, Jeanette. *Holy Invitations: Exploring Spiritual Direction*. Grand Rapids: Baker, 2000.

Benner, David G. *Sacred Companions: The Gift of Spiritual Friendship and Direction*. Downers Grove, Ill.: InterVarsity, 2002.

Doughety, Rose Mary. *Group Spiritual Direction: Community for Discernment*. New York: Paulist, 1995.

Edwards, Tilden. *Spiritual Director, Spiritual Companion: Guide to Tending the Soul*. New York: Paulist, 2001.

Guenther, Margaret. *Holy Listening: The Art of Spiritual Direction*. Boston: Cowley, 1992.

Jones, Alan. *Exploring Spiritual Direction* (new ed.). Cambridge, Mass.: Cowley, 1999 (1st ed. published 1982).

Jones, W. Paul. *The Art of Spiritual Direction: Giving and Receiving Spiritual Guidance.* Nashville: Upper Room, 2002.

Leech, Kenneth. *Soul Friend: Spiritual Direction in the Modern World* (new rev. ed.). Harrisburg, Pa.: Morehouse, 2001 (1st ed. published 1977).

Moon, Gary, and David Benner, eds. *Spiritual Direction and the Care of Souls: A Guide to Christian Approaches and Practices.* Downers Grove, Ill.: InterVarsity, 2004.

Peterson, Eugene H. *Working the Angles: The Shape of Pastoral Integrity.* Grand Rapids: Eerdmans, 1987.

John David Walt is the vice president of community life and dean of the chapel at the Wilmore, Kentucky, campus of Asbury Theological Seminary. He holds an M.Div. degree from Asbury and a J.D. degree from the University of Arkansas School of Law. Rev. Walt joined the Asbury seminary administration in the fall of 2000. Prior to this, he was a teaching and preaching pastor at The Woodlands United Methodist Church in Houston. As part of Rev. Walt's work at Asbury, he is giving leadership to the development of a Center for Prayer and Spiritual Formation. The center seeks to connect students with the full range of prayer and spiritual formation resources available through the seminary community and beyond.

In addition to his experience at The Woodlands, Rev. Walt served as the minister of students at Central United Methodist Church in Fayetteville, Arkansas, from 1992 to 1994. During that same time period, he was an associate at the law firm of Burke and Eldridge in Fayetteville. He also served brief tours as an associate with Wright, Lindsey & Jennings Law Firm in Little Rock, and as a legislative aid for United States Senator David Pryor.

Rev. Walt is an ordained elder in the Texas Annual Conference of the United Methodist Church. He and his wife, Tiffani, also an Asbury seminary graduate, have two children, John David III and Mary Kathryn, and a third on the way.

10
Sabbath Time for Sabbath Workers
John David Walt

Rest in rest
Holy leisure
Airtight time
Sabbath,

Creation slowing
Eyes open
Ears hearing
Sabbath,

Sacred rhythms
Guiltless feasting
Heaven hugging
Sabbath,

Nothing doing
Nowhere going
Work unknowing
Sabbath.*

OUR SENSE OF TIME SIMULTANEOUSLY REVEALS THE MOST THEO-
logical and practical reality in life. In the seminary where I serve, meetings
devour my time. In a recent meeting with several students, I experienced
an interesting phenomenon. With an effort to avoid looking at my watch
again, I glanced down at the student's watch next to me. Though my stom-
ach assured me it was nearing lunchtime, his watch read almost six o'clock.
I looked at my watch again and then at his. Mine said almost noon and his
six. Had I unknowingly entered the twilight zone? What was the meaning
of this disparity? Was this guy living in another time zone, or was his watch
really slow or fast. As the meeting broke for lunch, I inquired about his
timekeeping. He replied with an obvious tone, "Noon is the *sixth* hour." He
added, "It's also six in the evening where I served as a missionary in Swazi-

*Composition by author.

land." This student practiced a deeply Christian way of keeping time. On the one hand, he ordered his days around the passion of Christ. On the other, time continually reminded him to intercede for those near to his heart though living far away.

Our sense of time simultaneously reveals the most theological and practical reality in life. How do you tell time? What is your primary time-piece? Watch or calendar? Daytimer or PDA? Franklin-Covey time management system or palm pilot software? Secular calendar or Christian calendar? Time remains the most egalitarian reality and precious commodity on earth. We all have the same amount, and yet none can get enough. We speak of managing time, saving time, wasting time, and even killing time as though time were something within our control. And yet in reality, nothing exists more outside our control than time. Note these well-worn cultural observations. In soap opera speak: "Like sands through the hourglass, so are the days of our lives." In 1970s speak: "If I could put time in a bottle." Hear hymn writer Isaac Watts: "Time like an ever rolling stream, soon bears us all away; we fly forgotten, as a dream dies at the opening day." Benjamin Franklin opined that time was money. Sixteen centuries ago Augustine posed the question: "What is time? Provided no one asks me, I know. If I want to explain it to an inquirer, I do not know."

We sing and speak and lament so much about it, an objective observer might mistake time as our God. At minimum, I would venture to name time as the primary idol of our age, a view glimpsed by others not that long ago:

> Indeed, the eighteenth century satirist Jonathan Swift suggested that clocks themselves were becoming gods of mercantile society. When Gulliver traveled to Lilliput, Swift recounted in his famous novel, the small inhabitants were puzzled by the ticking object that hung at his waist. "We conjecture," they reported, that "it is either some unknown Animal, or the God that he worships. . . . But we are more inclined to the latter Opinion, because he assured us that he seldom did any Thing without consulting it . . . and said it pointed out the Time for every Action of his Life."[1]

So much of our attention focuses on time that the wristband around our left arm is called a watch. Meanwhile, *Webster* defines "watch" first as a verb: "to keep vigil as a devotional exercise" and "to be attentive or vigilant." Only much later in the sixth definition is watch defined as a portable timepiece designed to be worn or carried. "It is a great irony that monasteries—the very institutions from which we can learn so much about the practice of receiving the day—were pioneers in the development and use of clocks. Because Benedictine monks were committed to praying at set hours during the course of each day, it was crucial to them to discover a way to call the community to prayer. And they did, inventing machines that governed the ringing of the clocca, or bells. When the clocca rang, they drew attention to the eternity of God and the brevity of human life."[2] The daily office is nothing more than a creative effort to make time an icon through which they saw and entered into the sufferings of Christ. How might we recover a sense of time whereby time itself leads us to be watchful of our God.

The psalmist observes, "Seventy years are given to us! Some may even reach eighty. But even the best of these years are filled with pain and trouble; soon they disappear, and we are gone." And then this prayer, "Teach us to make the most of our time, so that we may grow in wisdom" (Ps. 90:10, 12, NLT). A book on spiritual formation for pastors would be remiss without both theological and practical reflection on the nature of time. Persons in ministry desperately need to recover an understanding of time as a reality to receive and embrace rather than a commodity to manage and control. At the foundation of time rests the reality of Sabbath. The aim of this essay, with the help of others, is to unpack the idea of Sabbath. Steering clear of the legalistic debris of both Jewish and Christian history, my hope is to unfold the practice of Sabbath as the wisdom of God.

Celebrated Jewish theologian Abraham Heschel writes:

> Judaism teaches us to be attached to holiness in time. . . . The Sabbaths are our great cathedrals. . . . One of the most distinguished words in the Bible is the word qadosh, holy; a word which more than any other is representative of the mystery and majesty of the divine. Now what was the first holy object in the history of the world? . . . It is, indeed, a unique occasion at which the distinguished word qadosh is used for the first time: in the Book of Genesis at the end of the story of creation. How extremely significant is the fact that it is applied to time: "And God blessed the seventh day and made it holy." There is no reference in the record of creation to any object in space that would be endowed with the quality of holiness.[3]

Hence the people of God in all times and at all places have been commanded to remember the Sabbath and to keep it holy. From the root command come three primary words: "Remember," "Sabbath," and "Holy." Taking these three ideas I will outline a theology and practice of Sabbath keeping with the remainder of this essay.

"REMEMBER THE SABBATH AND KEEP IT HOLY . . ."

Part one of the epic trilogy *The Lord of the Rings* begins with a narrator speaking these haunting words: "Much that once was is no longer, for none now live who remember it." On a visit to our seminary, a Native North American friend recounted a hunting story from his childhood. As he and his father trekked deeper and deeper into the forest, he became very afraid they were lost. Every few moments his father would stop and look around, carefully studying the surroundings. After this had gone on a while, the son asked his father if they were lost. His father answered, "No, Son, we are not lost, because I have spent twice as much time paying attention to where we have been as to where we are going." The essence of remembering is paying attention to the journey along which one has traveled. The failure to remember inevitably leads to a deep sense of lostness and disorientation.

A couple of years ago, I toured the Yad Vashem Holocaust Museum in Jerusalem. From the seemingly obscure beginnings of the Arian movement through Hitler's rise to power and on to the systematic extermination of 6 million Jews, the museum aims to lead people on a pilgrimage of remembrance. As our tour ended in the small gift shop, I noticed a small sign near the exit with these hopeful words: "Remembrance is the secret to redemption." Entire histories are lost and recurring cycles of doom are repeated unless the past is faithfully remembered. Remembering keeps us narrated into the plotline of the larger story shaping our lives.

Is it any wonder the watchword of ancient Israel was "remember"? "Remember the former things, those of long ago; I am God, and there is no other; I am God, and there is none like me" (Isa. 46:9). Over and over again throughout the Hebrew Scriptures, the people of God remember their story: from Creation down the spiraling staircase of sin to Babel, along the nomadic highway with Abraham and Sarah, climbing Mount Moriah with Isaac, watering camels with Rebekah, wrestling at the river Jabok with Jacob, and surprising starving brothers with Joseph. From Passover's Exodus to Red Sea's deliverance to Sinai's commandments and through the long wandering wilderness of temptation toward the Jordan, Israel's chief calling is to remember the God of their story. Three times a year, the people of God drop everything and make a pilgrimage to Jerusalem to remember and reenact their story through festival celebrations. Every week they observe the Sabbath. Every seventh year is a Sabbath where debts are forgiven and even the land gets to rest. And at the culmination of seven cycles of seven years, they celebrate a Jubilee where land ownership reverts back to God. In the interest of remembering, the Israelites commemorate covenants, build altars, stack stones, feast at festivals, sing psalms, and celebrate Sabbaths. The careful work of poets, priests, and prophets all aim toward one end: Remembering the God of their story.

In the sixth chapter of the Book of Deuteronomy, a document constitutive of Israel's life and faith, are these words:

> Hear, O Israel: The LORD our God, the LORD is one. Love the LORD your God with all your heart and with all your soul and with all your strength. These commandments that I give you today are to be upon your hearts. Impress them on your children. Talk about them

when you sit at home and when you walk along the road, when you lie down and when you get up. Tie them as symbols on your hands and bind them on your foreheads. Write them on the doorframes of your houses and on your gates (*Deut. 6:4-9*).

Israel shows us worship as an epic journey of remembrance into the future. Sadly, the exilic epitaph written over Israel's demise also boils down to one word: "forgot." Yet in the wake of Israel's failure comes one who remembers the story and inhabits it with imaginative fulfillment. The unfolding of Christ's fulfillment in the pattern of Israel's failure offers a stunning portrait of remembrance. Baptism at the Jordan River remembers Israel's entry into the land of promise. Forty days of battling with the devil remembers Israel's 40-year wandering in the wilderness. Feeding the multitudes on the hillside remembers God's provision of manna in the desert. The Sermon on the Mount remembers Moses on Mount Sinai. On we could go to the Crucifixion itself, where the Exodus unfolds again when Jesus becomes the Paschal Lamb of God. In declaring a new covenant, Jesus offers the bread and the cup, saying, "Do this in remembrance of me."

The biblical idea of remembrance conveys a far deeper sense of meaning than the mere recall of past events:

> Usually when the scripture uses the terms "remember" and "remembrance" with respect to worship, it does not imply a mental process but a ritual process. At the Eucharist, we remember Jesus not by quietly thinking about him but by doing what he did: Taking bread and the cup; giving thanks over them; breaking the bread; giving the bread and cup to those who seek to be Christian disciples. This remembrance by doing rather than by cogitation falls under the Greek term anamnesis. Compare amnesia. Amnesia is the loss of memory. Anamnesis is literally "the drawing near of memory," the entrance into our own experience of that which otherwise would be locked in the past.[4]

"Remember the Sabbath and keep it holy." The whole of Sabbath keeping might be summarized in the single word "remember." Sabbath opens space week after week after week to remember God's story, which reorients our reality, renarrating us into the plot of redemption. Sabbath is God's way of etching remembrance into the "DNA" of time. The secret to Sabbath begins not in patterns of behavior but in practices of memory.

"REMEMBER THE *SABBATH* AND KEEP IT HOLY . . ."

Sabbath keeping leads to a radical reorientation around the revolutionary reality of a God-shaped universe and a Christ-centered life. The command to remember the Sabbath appears within the Ten Commandments. Martin Luther once said, "Who knows the 10 commandments perfectly knows the entire Scriptures." The Ten Commandments are listed in two places in the Bible, and both versions are virtually identical in format, except for one important difference—the rationale offered for keeping the Sabbath. Recall the Exodus account of the Sabbath commandment:

> Remember the Sabbath day by keeping it holy. Six days you shall labor and do all your work, but the seventh day is a Sabbath to the LORD your God. On it you shall not do any work, neither you, nor your son or daughter, nor your manservant or maidservant, nor your animals, nor the alien within your gates. *For in six days the LORD made the heavens and the earth, the sea, and all that is in them, but he rested on the seventh day.* Therefore the LORD blessed the Sabbath day and made it holy (*Exod. 20:8-11, emphasis added*).

Now look at the Deuteronomy edition of the Sabbath commandment:

> Observe the Sabbath day by keeping it holy, as the LORD your God has commanded you. Six days you shall labor and do all your work, but the seventh day is a Sabbath to the LORD your God. On it you shall not do any work, neither you, nor your son or daughter, nor your manservant or maidservant, nor your ox, your donkey or any of your animals, nor the alien within your gates, so that your manservant and maidservant may rest, as you do. *Remember that you were slaves in Egypt and that the LORD your God brought you out of there with a mighty hand and an outstretched arm.* Therefore the LORD your God has commanded you to observe the Sabbath day (*Deut. 5:12-15*).

Sabbath keeping, like a double-edged sword, cuts to the heart of Christian faith: creation and restoration. We keep Sabbath as imitators of God, who created in six days and rested on the seventh. The Sabbath rhythm teaches us to rest from the creative work of our lives in order to reestablish touch with the creative wonder of God. Author and mystic Dorothee Soelle reminds us that the original state of creation was not fallenness but blessedness. She writes about the practice of radical amazement: "I think that every discovery of the world plunges us into jubilation, a radical amazement that tears apart the veil of triviality. Nothing is to be taken for granted, least of all beauty!"[5]

We also keep Sabbath as a perpetual reminder of the horrors of slavery and the deliverance of God. For 400 years God's people worked as Egyptian slaves without a day off. The Sabbath rhythm teaches us to rest from the hard work of our lives that we might be reintroduced to freedom.

> Now what is the meaning of the Sabbath that was given to Israel? It relativizes the works of mankind, the contents of the six working days. It protects mankind from total absorption by the task of subduing the earth, it anticipates the distortion which makes work the sum and purpose of human life, and it informs mankind that he will not fulfill

his humanity in his relation to the world which he is transforming but only when he raises his eyes above, in the blessed, holy hour of communion with the Creator. . . . The essence of mankind is not work![6]

Sabbath keeping returns us to the Cross, where freedom flows from the blood of Jesus Christ. At the Cross we worship Jesus and are delivered from our propensity to become enslaved to created things. Paul exhorts the Church to live "in view of God's mercy" (Rom. 12:1). Sabbath keeping provides a rhythmic journey, pausing again and again at scenic overlooks to gaze upon the stunning vista of mercy and grace.

Matt Redman, in his recent book *Face Down*, captures the essence of it all with these words: "When our eyes are opened to the big picture, and we catch a greater glimpse of God, we are *awestruck*. The otherness of God, His wonderful mysteries, the view of the whole Christ, the song of creation and the sound of sheer silence all lead us in one direction—awe. Facedown worshippers found throughout scripture all have one thing in common—an awesome view of God."[7]

"REMEMBER THE SABBATH AND *KEEP IT HOLY . . .*"

I have served in ministry now for 14 years. Until recent times, Sabbath keeping has been a tremendous struggle. Why? Because my idea of Sabbath was bound in pragmatic and utilitarian motives. Once while teaching a seminar on this subject, a man raised his hand and in an irritating fashion queried me, "What's the point of all this theology and philosophy about time!" Like so many of us, he only wanted the bottom line: "How do I do it?" In reality, he wanted to know the secrets to having a better day off. For a dozen years, my practice of Sabbath was the quest for a productive day off. Citing the authority of Jesus' statement about Sabbath being for people and not the other way around, I claimed the day as "my time." It was free time, alone time, time for running errands and getting other needful stuff done, or a time to work on my personal to-do list. It began when I woke up, and ended at bedtime. As a person in ministry, it was next to impossible to take Sabbath on Sunday, so I elected Fridays. In reality, I bounced around through the week, and half the time the demands of work kept me from taking it at all. When a consistent day didn't work, I reasoned an occasional Sabbath retreat would suffice. After all, in the New Testament reality, Sabbath didn't have to be a day. It could be an "ethic." In retrospect, despite all my best efforts to fill Sabbath with refreshment, it proved only a brief escape from the stressful pace of life and ministry.

As the long, treadmill-like journey to burnout continued, I began to study and teach on the biblical idea of Sabbath. As they say, one teaches best what he or she needs most. Here is what I learned about keeping Sabbath holy:

Lesson No. 1: Sabbath is a consistent weekly observance of a day (24-hour period) of rest. Someone once said, "God created days, but people created hours." The psalmist prays, "Teach [me] to number [my] days aright, that [I] may gain a heart of wisdom" (Ps. 90:12). Perhaps Sabbaths never measured up for me before because they only amounted to 12 hours at best. In keeping with the notion of creation days in Gen. 1, Sabbath begins in the evening. "And there was evening, and there was morning—the second day" (v. 8). The evening to morning pattern unfolds a theological reality:

> This Hebrew evening/morning sequence conditions us to the rhythms of grace. We go to sleep, and God begins his work. As we sleep he develops his covenant. We wake and are called out to participate in God's creative action. We respond in faith, in work. But always grace is previous and primary. We wake into a world we didn't make, into a salvation we didn't earn. Evening: God begins, without our help, his creative day. Morning: God calls us to enjoy and share and develop the work he initiated.[8]

There is something profoundly refreshing about the first major act of the day being bedtime. Waking up ceases to be an exercise in "jump-starting" the day and becomes an "entering into" the work God has already begun.

Lesson No. 2: Sabbath needs a clearly defined beginning and ending. In traditional Jewish practice, the Sabbath begins at sundown on Friday with the lighting of a special candle and the recitation of a prayer. A well-constructed, experiential ritual declares reality like nothing else. Our family begins Sabbath either at the evening meal or as we put our children to bed. We gather around and light what we call the "Sabbath Candle," reserved only for this day each week. Together we say the "Sabbath Prayer" we composed:

> God give us your peace and cause us to rest.
> We cease from our labor. We seek for your best.
> Embracing each other we walk in your ways.
> We thank you for giving this new Sabbath day.

As the candle begins to flicker, I feel as though I've crossed the finish line on the week and am entering into a victory celebration. In like fashion, at bedtime the following day we enjoy a time of "Sabbath Shadows," where we playfully make hand-shadows on the wall from the light of the candle. The children wrestle over blowing out the candle, and we move into a new week of life and ministry.

Lesson No. 3: Sabbath is not preparation for the week ahead, but celebration of the week behind. Rest, in the typical way of thinking, prepares us for the next task. Rest leads to refueling:

> Aristotle says relaxation is not an end but is rather for the sake of activity; for the sake of gaining strength for new efforts. To the biblical

mind, however, labor is the means toward an end, and the Sabbath as a day of rest, as a day of abstaining from toil, is not for the purpose of recovering one's lost strength and becoming fit for the forthcoming labor. The Sabbath is a day for the sake of life. . . . It is not an interlude but the climax of living.[9]

Through her book *Keeping Sabbath Wholly*, Marva Dawn proves a treasured teacher on Sabbath. "Sabbath resting is a foretaste of eternal life. . . . For that reason part of our Sabbath celebration is a prayer that we might someday come to the fulfillment of the Sabbath. . . . when [our Sabbaths] are the climax of our weeks, we know a healthy anticipation of the ultimate rest, the time when Jesus will come to take us home."[10]

Lesson No. 4: Sabbath is not about don'ts and dos but rather about a wholistic way of being in God's presence. Unfortunately, much Sabbath practice throughout the ages revolves more around construing the meaning of the word "work" and misconstruing the meaning of the word "holy." Dawn helpfully outlines Sabbath as a day of four holy practices: ceasing, resting, feasting, and embracing.

Ceasing

Our word "Sabbath" derives from the Hebrew word *Shabbat*. It means cease. The starting point for Sabbath resides simply in stopping. "To cease working on the Sabbath means to quit laboring at anything that is work. Activity that is enjoyable and freeing and not undertaken for the purpose of accomplishment qualifies as acceptable for Sabbath time."[11]

Sabbath is a day to exalt being done with doing. One of the great temptations of Sabbath lies in trading one to-do list for another. Needful household projects and unfinished daily chores cry out for completion. While it feels satisfying to check these things off the list, to persist in doing them violates the spirit of ceasing. The subtlest distortions in self-worth creep in through the inability to feel good about oneself without accomplishment. Sabbath provides a tangible way of realizing that God loves us not because of what we do or accomplish. And this sets us free to love others in the same way.

Perhaps the supreme act of faith in our time would be to hide one's to-do list. To cease affirms faith that God's will isn't dependent on our doing; that the world will go on without our constant contributions. Remember Israel's wilderness season? They did not gather manna on the Sabbath, but they collected two-days worth on the preceding day. Ceasing reestablishes connection with the rhythm of creation weeks: six days on and one day off. As Sabbath begins, I put my briefcase, laptop computer, palm pilot, and anything else reminding me of work in a closet. Finally, I place my watch in a drawer and prepare to embrace Shabbat.

Resting

On the seventh day, having finished His task, God rested from all His work (Gen. 2:2). Pastor and theologian Eugene Peterson describes Sabbath as that uncluttered time and space in which we can distance ourselves from our own activities enough to see what God is doing. He suggests if we are not able to rest one day a week, we may be taking ourselves far too seriously.[12] The psalmist reminds us to "Be still, and know that I am God" (Ps. 46:10). Throughout the centuries, rabbis have speculated that God created rest on the seventh day. "What was created on the seventh day. 'Tranquility, serenity, peace and repose'" (Genesis rabba 10:9).

Martin Luther, speaking on Sabbath, said, "The spiritual rest which God especially intends in this commandment is that we not only cease from our labor and trade but much more—that we let God alone work in us and that in all our powers do we do nothing of our own."[13] Rather than succumbing to the temptation to define rest, it must be left to the creative imagination of individuals, families, and communities. Finding rest can easily become a tiring activity in itself, for one person's rest is another's tiring activity. True rest resides in the province of surrender. Like green pastures and still waters, real rest deeply restores and is a place to which only God can lead.

Wendell Berry captures the essence of Sabbath in his poetry.

The mind that comes to rest is tended
In ways that it cannot intend:
Is borne, preserved, and comprehended
By what it cannot comprehend
Your Sabbath, Lord, thus keeps us by
Your will, not ours. And it is fit
Our only choice should be to die
Into that rest, or out of it.[14]

Dawn summarizes, "The Sabbath rhythm of resting leads to an ethics of becoming (how our character is being developed) and not of doing (how we react in specific situations). . . . Resting provides the necessary time for the Spirit's molding of our characters."[15]

Feasting

Every Sabbath morning our family enjoys a feast. After a few cups of coffee, our children, 4 and 2, begin chanting, "Sabbath pancakes, Sabbath pancakes!" Ordinary pancakes, through ritual celebration, have become an extraordinary feast. So special have pancakes become that once when a baby-sitter tried to cook pancakes on a weekday morning, our two-year-old insisted that pancakes were only for the Sabbath.

Feasting, a lost art in our culture of abundance, has become primarily about eating more. The essence of feasting is not quantity but quality. But we cannot talk about feasting without a discussion on fasting. A day set apart for the unbridled enjoyment of special foods invites a new understanding of fasting in the week. Because our idea of feasting is quantity-driven, so is our practice of fasting. After all, if feasting implies "all you can eat," then fasting demands complete abstinence. But what if fasting moved beyond either-or categories? Might we be led away from our "living to eat" idolatry, joining the rest of the world in an "eating to live" lifestyle. Our everyday diet could become a form of fasting whereby we stood in solidarity with those whose diet is not about choice but scarcity. I dream of our seminary's lunch offering as a free soup line and an opportunity to make an offering benefiting the poor. So much of our time is wasted on deciding where to eat and then what to eat when we get there. Food commands our focus because it delivers a ready alternative to fill our emptiness. Feasting enables one to embrace the living God in the gift of provision, no matter its quality or quantity.

Getting beyond food, feasting invites guilt-free enjoyment of everything beautiful. Dawn develops the idea of feasting on affection where we enjoy solitude with God, community with friends, and intimacy in marriage. Sabbath affords me space to read and write poetry, supplying a feast of beauty. Finally, Sabbath reminds us bread alone will never satisfy the appetite that craves feasting on the Word of God.

Embracing

"Tell the people of Israel to keep my Sabbath day, for the Sabbath is a sign of the covenant between me and you forever" (Exod. 31:13, NLT). To celebrate Sabbath is to embrace the Triune God of grace.

> Most of the days of the week we do . . . what is expected of us. Sabbath keeping frees us . . . to uncork our own spontaneity. Because there is nothing we have to do, we are suddenly free . . . to discover the presence of God hidden all around us. To keep the Sabbath invites us to have festival fun, to play, to enjoy our guests and our activities, to relish the opportunity for worship, to celebrate the eternal presence of God himself. . . . Our bodies, minds, souls, and spirits celebrate together with others that God is in our midst.[16]

Through ceasing, resting, and feasting, Sabbath teaches us the art of embracing. It is the indistinguishable love of God and neighbor.

"When Jews who have become inattentive to their religion wish to deepen their observance, rabbis tell them with one voice: You must begin by keeping *Shabbat*. . . . 'more than the Jews have kept *Shabbat*, *Shabbat* has kept the Jews.'"[17] Eugene Peterson, in a letter written to his congregation, warns us all,

The world is in a conspiracy to steal our Sabbath. It is a pick-pocket kind of theft (nothing like an armed robbery) and we aren't aware of it until long after its occurrence. The "world" is sometimes our friends, sometimes our families, sometimes our employers—they want us to work for them, not waste time with God, not be our original selves. If the world can get rid of Sabbath, it has us to itself. What it does with us when it gets us is not very attractive: after a few years of Sabbath breaking we are passive consumers of expensive trash, and anxious hurriers after fantasy pleasures. We lose our God and our dignity at about the same time. That is why I want you to keep a Sabbath. Guard the day. Protect the leisure for praying and playing.[18]

Sabbath gracefully reconnects us to God in a magnificent storied fashion. Jurgen Moltmann says, "The Sabbath opens creation to its true future."[19] The Sabbath may be the central design in the tapestry of time. It is at minimum the wisdom of God. Let us, therefore, labor to, "Remember the Sabbath and keep it holy."

Notes

1. Dorothy Bass, *Receiving the Day: Christian Practices for Opening the Gift of Time* (Indianapolis: Jossey-Bass, 2001), 26.

2. Ibid.

3. Abraham Joshua Heschel, *The Sabbath: Its Meaning for Modern Man* (New York: Farrar, Straus and Giroux, 1951), 8-9.

4. Laurence Hull Stookey, *Calendar: Christ's Time for the Church* (Nashville: Abingdon Press, 1996), 29.

5. Dorothee Soelle, *The Silent Cry: Mysticism and Resistance* (Minneapolis: Augsburg Fortress, 2001), 89.

6. Henri Blocher, *In the Beginning* (Downers Grove, Ill.: InterVarsity Press, 1984), 57.

7. Matt Redman, *Face Down (The Worship Series)* (Ventura, Calif.: Regal Books, 2004), 90.

8. Eugene Peterson, "The Pastor's Sabbath," *Leadership* (Spring 1985), 53.

9. Heschel, *The Sabbath*, 14.

10. Marva Dawn, *Keeping Sabbath Wholly* (Grand Rapids: Eerdmans, 1989), 62.

11. Ibid., 5.

12. Peterson, "The Pastor's Sabbath," 55-56. Quoted in Dawn, *Keeping Sabbath Wholly*, 70.

13. Martin Luther, *A Treatise on Good Works* (Philadelphia: A. J. Holman Company, 1915), 173-285, part 2, xvii.

14. Wendell Berry, *A Timbered Choir: The Sabbath Poems* (New York: Counterpoint Press, 1999), 7.

15. Dawn, *Keeping Sabbath Wholly*, 96-97.

16. Ibid., 202.

17. Dorothy Bass, *Practicing Our Faith: A Way of Life for a Searching People* (Indianapolis: Jossey-Bass, 1998), 79-80.

18. "Confessions of a Former Sabbath Breaker," *Christianity Today* (Sept. 2, 1988).

19. Jurgen Moltmann, *God in Creation* (Minneapolis: Fortress Press, 1993), 276.

Marjorie J. Thompson is an ordained minister in the Presbyterian Church U.S.A. She received her B.A. in religious studies from Swarthmore College and her M.Div. from McCormick Theological Seminary. Following a pastoral internship, she became a research fellow at Yale Divinity School, where she studied Christian spirituality with Henri Nouwen and did independent research in the ecumenical traditions of prayer. Marjorie has served as adjunct faculty for several seminaries, including McCormick and Vanderbilt Divinity School. In 1996, she began working with Upper Room Ministries where she served as chief architect of a major new resource in congregational small-group formation called Companions in Christ. She is now designated as director of Pathways in Congregational Spirituality. Marjorie has written articles for two of the sequel resources in the Companions Series on forgiveness and the Beatitudes. She is also author of *Family: The Forming Center* and *Soul Feast: An Invitation to the Christian Spiritual Life.*

11
Making Choices:
Developing a Personal Rule of Life
Marjorie J. Thompson

❧ ONE OF THE ELDERS OF THE DESERT TRADITION SAID, "THE reason why we do not get anywhere is that we do not know our limits, and we are not patient in carrying out the work we have begun. But without any labor at all we want to gain possession of virtue."[1] These words are worth pondering as church leaders. How many of us know our own limits? I suspect few of us know either our true limitations or capabilities, because we have not really tested ourselves in full reliance on God's grace. Few of us persevere patiently in our spiritual practices until they yield their deepest gifts. In our increasingly "quick fix" culture we want virtue without labor, transformation without effort, and new life without dying.

Our hearts swim in the restless tide of the world around us, by turns complacent and dissatisfied. We are ambivalent about letting go of old habits to make room for new ones. Divided in mind, we become diluted in spirit. Our prayers are intermittent, our desire for God lukewarm, and our love for others hot and cold.

We need desperately to be centered. Our souls crave a unified vision, a clear focus, and unapologetic priorities. Such clarity of purpose and integration of energy is the reason for a rule of life. What is at stake is the reach of our spiritual maturity, the authenticity of our leadership in the church.

A RULE OF LIFE

"Rule of life" is not generally familiar language to Protestants. Historically a rule of life was a documented set of commitments describing the spiritual disciplines that bound together a monastic community. Such rules remain active today, the best known being the Rule of Benedict (6th century A.D.). As the concepts of spiritual formation have taken root in contemporary Protestant churches, many individuals have chosen to frame a personal "rule of life," recording the spiritual practices they intend to live by.

139

A personal rule of life is a way of ordering our lives to catch the wind of grace. It is not a matter of practicing 3 or 4 or 10 disciplines as a spiritual self-improvement project. A rule represents a whole way of life, an integrated orientation toward God involving our perceptions, attitudes, and habits of thought, word, and action in the world.

Particular spiritual disciplines are chosen to help us reframe our lives around God. A dear colleague[2] is fond of recalling how his family, vacationing on a remote island in the North Woods, once had a chance to see the great northern lights. They discovered that the best way to see the lights was to lie flat on their backs on the dock. My friend pointed out that spiritual disciplines are ways we *position* ourselves to notice divine grace so we may learn to respond to it more freely.

A personal rule of life is tailor-made. Of course it is helpful to see the variety of rules that communities and individuals have devised over time. We can catch a vision of what a spiritually mature life looks like, noting that it includes humility, compassion, patience, courage, trust, and good humor. Such a vision can help shape what we become. But what we cannot do is live another's life. No matter how excellent, another's life will not fit us. Martin Buber recounts the comment of an old Hasidic rabbi named Zusya just before his death: "In the world to come, they will not ask me: why were you not Moses? They will ask me: Why were you not Zusya?"[3]

If we try to imitate another too closely, we are merely role-playing, living an alienated life. I have come to think that the "midlife crisis" is essentially a crisis of authenticity. We are deciding if it is possible to come out from behind the smokescreen of our *persona* or expected role. We are testing whether or not to be who we really are—or more aptly—to allow ourselves to become real by God's grace. A rule of life gives us a way of allowing God's love to "make us real."

If we really want to mature, we need to do three things: (1) take stock of our spiritual life as it now is, for better or worse; (2) discern what we need in order to progress toward a deeper experience of communion with God; and (3) make choices about intentional practices we can actually live with.

Taking Stock: A Faith-Illumined Inventory

God's grace comes to us in ways uniquely suited to our character and circumstances. One could say that grace is always context-specific. In order to discern the spiritual practices we are called to, we need first to pay close attention to our own context. One way to begin is by taking "a faith-illumined inventory of our lives."[4] Ask yourself: What are my actual life circumstances and commitments? What is my character and personality? What are my gifts and weaknesses? Your answers to such questions provide the key to how your rule of life will be (and already is to some extent) shaped and structured.

You can do this inventory systematically. Start with your primary relationships. Are you married? If so, you have made vows before God and the whole community of faith to live in a certain way with your spouse. You have promised to be faithful in marriage; to support and care for one another in good times and bad; and to love each other, pray for each other, and grow with each other. This is no small matter in a personal rule. Indeed, your marriage commitments are a crucial dimension of your rule of life.

Do you have children? It has been wryly observed that raising children is an automatic invitation to asceticism! Those of you with children have learned, many times over, to release your own agenda for the sake of your children's needs. You have let go of some of your most cherished dreams to make room for your children's dreams. You have given away your youth in the wear and tear of rearing little ones, and perhaps struggled with a few demons in the process of parenting adolescents. Everything that goes into giving your children a solid foundation in life—the security of love, the clarity of healthy boundaries, affirmation for gifts, encouragement for aspirations, consolation in disappointment, and the example of a living faith they may choose to share—is integral to your rule of life.

Do you care for aging parents? Do you hold deep friendships as dear to you as family, or have collegial relationships that require particular attention? Do you consider your work a calling from God? The same basic principle applies. Your actual lived commitments are key elements in your rule of life. They constitute the shape of your personal mission from God in the world at this time. Your rule simply states how you choose to express these relationships and tasks.

Let me suggest that you take a few minutes for a simple exercise here and now. List briefly what you consider essential among your current life commitments and responsibilities. Then note particular choices you have already made in how you live these out.

When you have completed this exercise, the question shifts: How do these commitments fit your own character and personality? For in addition to your actual circumstances and commitments, you must factor in who you are. Three questions can guide us here. First: *What are your personal gifts and graces?* Are you energetic, organized, reliable, imaginative, sensitive, courageous, clear thinking, humorous? Do you have musical, relational, or manual intelligence?[5] Second: *What are your weaknesses and limitations?* Do you have limited energies, physically or emotionally? Do you give up easily, lack confidence, or suffer from cynicism? Are you impatient, quick-tempered, an inveterate procrastinator, a perfectionist, or too eager to please others? Third: *What is your personality, your style?* Are you introverted or extroverted, a "morning person" or a "night owl"? Do you like clear structure and regular habits, or prefer spontaneity and variation?

Discerning What We Need to Grow

Having made a start on a faith-illumined inventory—taking stock of the actual commitments and characteristics of our lives—we are now in a position to discern what is needed for further spiritual growth.

Most of us by now are familiar with the Myers-Briggs Type Indicator (MBTI). It is commonplace to identify ourselves as introverts or extraverts in explaining certain personal habits or felt needs. In relation to spiritual practices, we tend to accept that introverts need solitude and quiet to sustain their spirits, while extraverts find renewed strength through interaction with others. Indeed, each of the four sets of preferences in the MBTI can help us choose appropriate spiritual practices. A "sensing" type seeks sensory expression. This might include the use of candlelight, incense, visual aids to prayer, or a walk through the beauty of nature to restore the soul. A sensing person is also likely to seek concrete expressions of faith through action as a physical embodiment of prayer. An "intuiting" person will find greater meaning in symbolic and metaphorical expressions of faith. This might mean pondering scripture texts with the heart attuned to images that shape spiritual insight. It might involve gazing on icons or other symbolic representations of faith, seeking their inner meaning; or walking a labyrinth in a meditative frame of mind. A "thinking" type needs study, seeking a certain amount of knowledge as a basis for reflecting on the meaning of faith. Thinking persons often need to see concrete applications of spiritual realities to daily life as well. The "feeling" type seeks inspiration. This is a heartfelt spirituality that loves hymn singing and warm fellowship. Much Evangelical worship and praise is expressive of the feeling personality type.[6]

While it is important to pay attention to who we are and to what comes naturally as spiritual nourishment, we need also to reflect on what would bring *balance* to our lives. God calls us to grow by drawing us beyond our comfort zones, stretching us to develop the nondominant side of our personality. Sometimes we are inclined to use the dominant parts of ourselves—those in which we feel confident and secure—to control, manipulate, or judge. Thus, because it is natural for us, we assume it should be so for others. Or we denigrate the less dominant parts of ourselves: If I am a thinking type, I may dismiss my feelings as "mere sentimentality"; if I am a feeling type, I may judge my intellect with suspicion and label it "head-tripping." We need to learn that all facets of personality are in fact part of our own psychological makeup, however recessive some may be. Balance brings wholeness and integration to our personality.

Sometimes the practice we need has little to do with personality and everything to do with our relational commitments and stage of life. Perhaps we see clearly what we need in order to grow spiritually, but the way we choose to go about it does not fit our circumstances.

Gerald May, of the Shalem Institute, tells this story of his early efforts to practice centering prayer, a form of prayer to which he felt deeply called. He had a wife and young children when, in his reasoned wisdom, he thought the best time for the two daily 20-minute practices would be while the children were getting ready for school in the morning, and while his wife was getting dinner ready in the evening. One evening, while he was getting peacefully settled into his prayer on the porch outside the kitchen, a large fish came flying out the window. As the fish slapped into Jerry's face, he heard his wife's voice saying, "I hope you meditate your silly brains out!" They are still married. Jerry learned that "there is a time for every purpose under heaven" but not always the time you think!

Truly, "for everything there is a season." If you are in the season of changing diapers, you can choose to allow it to be a spiritual awakening. One of my mentors, a former Trappist monk turned Episcopal priest, now married, with two adopted children, speaks of "contemplation amid every form of baby effluent." If you are in a season of advanced schooling, your studies are part of your current spiritual practice. Those in the season of the empty nest are engaged in the essential spiritual practice of letting go. If you are undergoing a season of congregational or marital strife, ask yourself what spiritual practice this might be inviting you to. A season of ill health can be an opportunity to practice trust, visualize restored health, or intercede for those sicker than you. Indeed, many kinds of personal affliction may provide a doorway to offer on behalf of others our suffering as a way of participating in the mystery of Christ's redemptive suffering for all.

The seasons of our lives are wonderful teachers in helping us discern the specific aspects of a rule of life. So finally we come to the core: making choices we can live with and live in.

Making Choices We Can Live With

A personal rule of life is more than certain forms of prayer, journaling, or devotional reading. It has as much to do with attitudes and perceptions carried into the daily round of activities as with particular exercises of faith. For example, the Rule of Benedict stresses growing in humility and obedience. Pope John Paul the 23rd made a habit of turning his mind to God frequently during the day. When Martin Luther King Jr. laid out the principles all civil rights protesters had to subscribe to, it represented a way of life, including key commitments of attitude and behavior—refraining from violence of mind, word, or fist, and walking and talking in the manner of love, since God is love.

A significant part of any rule of life, then, is the intentional cultivation of Spirit-guided attitudes, perceptions, and responses. For example, we can choose to see the best in each other, recognizing and encouraging potential wherever possible rather than just criticizing weakness. How often at home do we ask our children or spouse to focus on what they did wrong rather than on what they did right? Given the power of thoughts, words, and imagination to evoke the reality they dwell on, this can be a self-defeating habit. Is praise and appreciation for the good we see in each other part of our rule of life, both at home and at work?

What about guarding our thoughts and judgments, seeking grace in the present moment, and cultivating gratitude? These aspects of a personal rule are not dependent on practices that require set-aside times; rather they bring a mind and heart attuned to God into daily life.

My own rule of life has changed significantly over the years in this regard. I used to practice more time-specific disciplines, such as silent retreats, spiritual reading, scriptural meditation, journaling with dreams, fasting, and daily prayers with my husband. During the 10 years I did this, I worked at home, engaging in freelance retreat work, teaching, and writing. Over the past 8 years, my life has changed substantially in work patterns, scheduling, and home commitments. Now I find myself practicing what I would call "vigilance over thoughts." Ancient Christian hermits used this phrase to describe guarding the heart from sinful thoughts or distractions in prayer. For me it has broad application. It means an intentional effort to see God's image in every person I see and to refrain from hasty judgments. It means expressing gratitude in advance, anticipating the appearance of divine blessing. It means looking for grace and humor in situations that seem devoid of them. This is not easy for me. Vigilance over thoughts represents a true discipline of cultivating new habits.

Several years ago, I was forcibly struck by an article written by Robert Morris in the journal *Weavings*. Never had I seen expressed so clearly the nature of the change I had been experiencing in my own rule of life. Morris began by admitting that he never had much success implementing a daily practice of prayer. His life just seemed too episodic and unpredictable to "carve out the space" for a steady, satisfying prayer life. But one day, rushing and behind schedule, he stubbed his toe on the stairs and exclaimed in frustration: "O God!" Then he paused:

> O God? . . . I mused, toe still throbbing. *That's a prayer! Well, if I'm praying, why not go all the way?* So, on the next conscious breath, I breathed more deeply and repeated, in a somewhat more friendly groan, "O God!" On the third breath I heard myself pray, with more feeling, "O God . . . bless." That one word, *bless,* evoked a cascade of

feelings: *Bless my aching toe. Bless by ruffled spirits. Bless my frazzled body. Bless me in my heedless rush.*[7]

Morris observed that his "search for a daily prayer discipline had finally found the place to set up practice"—right in the midst of daily frustrations. He saw that our sputtering, judging reactions to the unpredictable turns of life are precisely an occasion for spiritual practice; that the impulse to make exasperated exclamations such as "O God!" is, however imperfectly, an impulse to pray, and that we can choose to turn these utterances to blessings if we see the opportunity. He points out quite disarmingly that "the way you live your life *is* your spiritual practice."[8]

One way to describe what Morris discovered was a basic movement from a *time-based* model of spiritual discipline to an *event-based* daily spiritual practice. Instead of setting aside specific times for prayer, spiritual reading, or retreat, he found in the flow of daily events regular reminders to live in a prayerful stance.

That shift from time- to event-based spiritual practice named part of what I had been experiencing in my own life. Of course, claiming such a shift can simply become an excuse for failing to set spiritual priorities in the midst of a busy life. In truth, we need a certain familiarity with time-based practices before we can become sufficiently conscious of the spiritual opportunities that lie within daily events. Moreover, to respond faithfully to daily occasions requires drawing on specific practices learned during times set apart: the use of short prayers, scripture or song phrases, visualizing the light of God surrounding a person or situation.

Time-based and event-based spiritual practices are complementary and mutually reinforcing. We are unlikely to get far with perceptual and attitudinal shifts unless we have at least a periodic immersion in classic, time-based spiritual practices.

Establishing Our Personal Rule

When it comes to establishing our actual commitments in a personal rule of life, there are two basic approaches. One we could call an ascetic approach; the other a mystical approach. They will need some balancing since they require one another. The ascetic approach basically asks, *What do I need to let go of?* The mystical approach asks, *What do I need to take up?*

The ascetic dimension of a rule of life invites us to consider what separates us from God, and asks us to give it up. What prevents us from reflecting the goodness and beauty of God's image? What gets in the way of our spiritual communion and joy? A habit of self-denigration? Fearing the worst? An eating or spending habit?

If eating habits are a block to your spiritual freedom, look at your particular situation. Not everyone should fast, nor in the same way. It may be that attending to your salt and fat intake is the particular form fasting needs to take for you. If shopping is a compulsion, perhaps removing easy access to credit cards can help you deal with it. I have a friend who has frozen her credit card in an ice tray! It's not impossible to get at, but to do so requires effort and sufficient time to reconsider her impulses. She also puts all her mail order catalogs in a box with a lock on it. That way she can get at them if she chooses, but they are not simply strewn about the house inviting perusal.

The mystical dimension of a rule of life invites us to consider what practices will open us to the divine mystery more fully. Ask yourself, What way of prayer or life draws me deeper into the experience of God's presence, grace, and love? What invites me to intimacy with God in a gracious way, yet also challenges me to be open to God's claim upon my life? Is there a form of prayer, such as walking meditation, that attracts me? Does imaginative prayer help me enter the Gospels and find myself encountered by the living Christ? Or do I need to walk with God into the local soup kitchen and find Christ's presence in "the least of these"?

As with all spiritual practices, the real question is what gives you more life, abundant life! Whether letting go or taking on, it is to make room for the divine life God is breathing into you. We are aiming to receive the love of God so deeply that we can begin to love God, others, and ourselves with God's love. The ultimate rule of life for any person of faith is the Golden Rule: Love.

When you have considered your options—what draws you, what you need for balance, where you might be stretched—then frame your rule of life. Take into account that you already have a rule by virtue of your current life commitments. Choose just a few new practices, maybe two or three. Don't get carried away by enthusiasm for changing your habits. Maybe only one new discipline is called for in your life right now. Far better to start small and let your practice grow as the Spirit urges, than to start grandiose, fail, and fall by the wayside yet again. Some of us set ourselves up for failure like this every New Year. Be faithful in a few small things. Then watch the garden grow!

Sustaining Our Personal Rule

Even with a modest rule of life you can expect to trip up often. Instead of getting distressed by this, be gentle with yourself. You are learning to walk in a particular way, just like a toddler. Thomas Merton once wisely noted that in spiritual matters we will be beginners all of our lives.[9] Accept this. You will fall often, but just get up and start again. Someone once observed, "It's not falling in the water that drowns us but staying there."[10] If you insist on judging and punishing yourself for skipping your practice or failing to be gracious, you will slow your progress down. Instead of dwelling on what you haven't done and expending energy feeling guilty, just breathe a simple prayer of confession, ask for God's help, and start again. God is extraordinarily generous.

There are four things you can do to help yourself live your commitments: (1) Persevere in your practice: just as a tree cannot get rooted if it is continually transplanted, so we cannot get rooted firmly in the soil of God's love if we are constantly changing our practice. (2) Find support for your rule from at least two other persons of faith, and preferably from a larger community. You won't make it on your own. History is littered with the spiritual dry bones of aspiring Lone Rangers. (3) Stay open to the Spirit with regard to possible revisions of your rule over time. Sometimes we do not discern well what truly fits us, and we need a midcourse correction; sometimes our lives change significantly enough to require a change in our rule. (4) Finally, seek God's grace to be faithful to your practice. Ask for grace to persevere, to find support, and to discern needed changes. Grace is the ultimate key to any success in the life of the spirit.

May God bless you with abundant grace for the journey!

Notes

1. Thomas Merton, *The Wisdom of the Desert* (New York: New Directions Books, 1960), 34.

2. Rueben Job, retired United Methodist bishop and author.

3. Martin Buber, *Tales of the Hasidim: Early Masters* (New York: Schocken Books, 1975), 251.

4. A felicitous phrase borrowed from my friend and colleague, the Rev. William Wilson.

5. The groundbreaking work of Howard Gardner on multiple intelligences lies behind these categories. Gardner proposes seven types of intelligence, including bodily-kinesthetic, spatial, musical, interpersonal, and intrapersonal in addition to standard linguistic and logical-mathematical categories. See *Frames of Mind: The Theory of Multiple Intelligences*, 2nd ed. (New York: Basic Books, 1993).

6. For a more nuanced and comprehensive interpretation of MBTI in relation to spirituality, see Michael and Norrisey, *Prayer and Temperament* (The Open Door, 1984); also Kiersey and Bates, *Please Understand Me* (Prometheus Nemesis Books, 1978).

7. "The Second Breath," *Weavings, A Journal of the Christian Spiritual Life* (Mar.-Apr. 1998), 37.

8. Ibid., 38.

9. Merton writes, "We do not want to be beginners. But let us be convinced of the fact that we will never be anything else but beginners, all our life!" See *Contemplative Prayer* (Image Books, 1971), 37.

10. Source unknown.

APPENDIX: QUESTIONS FOR DISCERNMENT

Below are some practical questions to consider as you work on formulating a personal rule. Review them and reflect on the ones that "call your name."

1. How do I currently live my spiritual life? (Be honest; there's no one to fool but yourself.)

2. What is satisfying about my spiritual life? What is unsatisfying or frustrating?

3. What has been most helpful to me in the past? Is it still helpful, or does my practice seem to be changing? How?

4. What particular practice(s) do I feel especially drawn to right now? (Could be classic or quite unconventional—baking, chopping wood, playing with children)

5. Where do I need *balance* in my life? What would give it to me?

6. What would it look like to be more *open* to God in my life? What would help?

7. What would help me to be more *faithful* to God?

8. What would help *focus* my life on what is most important to me spiritually?

Bill Hybels is founder and senior pastor at Willow Creek Community Church in South Barrington, Illinois. Hybels has authored 17 books, including *Courageous Leadership* and *The Volunteer Revolution*. He also serves as chairman of the Willow Creek Association, a fellowship of over 10,500 like-minded churches worldwide. He received his degrees from Trinity College in Deerfield, Illinois. Bill and Lynne are the parents of two grown children, Shauna and Todd.

12
Bold Love:
Magnetic Attraction for Seekers and Believers
Bill Hybels

❦ SOME WONDER WHAT GOES ON BEHIND THE SCENES AT WILLOW Creek Community Church. Because love stands at the center of our message, we want our staff relationships to experience and model Christian love. Willow Creek is a church, a biblically functioning community, where bold love is given and received. We believe bold love impacts ministry and sets a healthy emotional climate for satisfaction in service.

For example, staff members still slide notes under each other's door. Let me share smatterings of notes I have received from fellow team members. One ends this way: "I cannot imagine doing ministry without your understanding and friendship. This event has been another peak experience for me, which I will treasure for a long time. I absolutely love doing this redemptive adventure with you."

Another note read: "Bill, thank you. What you are doing this week is such a beautiful thing to behold. God is doing it again. He is filling you up with His energy, words, vision, and strength. Your loving friend in Christ."

Such notes are not out of the ordinary. There is a steady flow of loving interaction and support between us here at Willow Creek.

I write about as many notes as I receive. Certainly I cannot speak authoritatively about all concentric circles around Willow Creek Community Church, but loving attitudes and deeds are becoming standard fare where I operate. This work of God at Willow Creek goes forward with love, acceptance, and grace. That's as it should be, and that's what we want.

CATCHING UP AND ENJOYING IT

I regret that it took me half of my ministry life to wake up to the supremacy of love. I memorized 1 Cor. 13 as a kid. Many Christian leaders know these passages extremely well: "Love is patient, love is kind, and is not jealous; love does not brag and is not arrogant, does not act unbecomingly; it does not seek its own, is not provoked. . . . [Love] bears all things, believes all things, hopes all things, endures all things. Love never fails. . . . But the greatest of these is love" (vv. 4-5, 7-8, 13, NASB). I cannot explain why it took so long for me to understand the message of that incredible passage of Scripture. But I am now catching up and enjoying it.

Jesus taught us that love will be the main measuring rod by which our lives will be assessed. On days when I think clearly, I realize I do not want to be remembered as a person of vision, or one who achieved great goals, or one who led a big church. I would much rather be remembered by my wife, children, friends, and the flock of God as being a person with an extraordinary capacity to love. Great pastors love people.

Here's an example that underscores my point. It is the kind of thing we try to notice at Willow Creek. We like to validate examples of love. John Ortberg, who served as a teaching pastor for nine years, started to describe the last four steps in a seven-step strategy, but one of the props was out of order. As he spoke, I thought, "Props are goofed up. John's hung. Oh, no." I knew John was going to be surprised when he turned around. Then I thought, "Oh, if he makes a biting comment about how someone messed up, there's going to be embarrassment and hurt feelings." But when John noticed the visuals were out of order, he laughed and said, "You are just trying to test me, aren't you?" He gave a soft, affectionate answer without blame.

When I saw him later, I said, "John, your reply was classy and loving. Instead of making a stinging comment, you turned it around and had fun with it. You protected the crew who are working hard to help you. And listeners saw through a window into your soul that you are a loving man." Such a response can only come from a loving leader who is committed to developing loving people.

Once we had a conference when one of our vocalists was up singing. In the middle of the song a disturbed attender whose medication was a little unbalanced left the congregation, climbed on the platform, and stood next to her. It was an uncomfortable moment for everyone.

Though the vocalist did not understand what was happening, she simply changed hands with her microphone, put her arm around this troubled young woman, finished the song, and walked off with her new friend by her side. This simple act communicated the power of love and acceptance.

SETTING THE RELATIONAL TEMPERATURE

Nothing compares with love among believers. An expanded capacity to love is the best gift you can give your church and family. It can revolutionize your ministry, attract new people, and enrich your own life.

Let me say it again—I was in church work a long time before I awakened to the fact that love has to be fundamentally what I am about and what the church is about. I need to continually increase my capacity to give and receive love. As pastor, I need to set the relational temperature of the amount of love that flows in the circles of my influence. I have to increase my capacity to give and receive love and express it inside and outside the church. And I must take responsibility for setting a loving temperature in the church.

ESTABLISHING INTENTIONAL REGIMEN

All of this means that since Jesus gave us the Great Commandment to love God with all our heart, soul, mind, and strength, and to love our neighbor as ourselves, then we must increase our capacity to give and receive love. We need an intentional program for increasing love just as we need a workout regimen to be muscularly or cardiovascularly healthy. We need a plan to develop greater hearts of love toward our people.

If I asked you, "What is your plan for increasing your capacity to give and receive love," how would you answer? If love is the greatest, if love is what God wants more than anything else, and if the world needs more love—what is your workout plan to make it happen? What is your strategic plan to increase love in your life and church? Let me share some issues I am working on for my own life.

DRINK OFTEN FROM THE FOUNTAIN OF GOD'S LOVE

If my capacity for giving and receiving love is to increase, I have to regularly drink from the fountain of the love of God. Remember the passage that says, "We love because he first loved us" (1 John 4:19)? That teaches that I am never going to increase my love capacity until I increase my capacity to receive love from God. I think about this a lot. How can I drink more effectively from the fountain of the love of God?

This is painstakingly practical. To get me closer to God's love, I listen to worship music CDs. There are mornings when I know I am overcommitted at the start of the day. Sometimes I know it is going to be a rush from 5:30 A.M. until 10 that night. When I think maybe I have bitten off too much, I remind myself that I am likely to be dangerous by about 10 or 11 A.M. My RPMs will be too high. I will be short with people. I will speak too fast. I am going to say, "Give me the bottom line." I know where that takes me because I have been there before. I realize I will bruise people if I do it that way.

So to get my day started right, I must drink from the fountain of the love of God. I have a small sound system in my office and a bunch of CDs. I put my feet up on the credenza, lean back in my chair, put in a worship CD, and I drink from the fountain of the love of God.

Another source for me are the writings of Henri Nouwen. I have bought nearly everything he has written. I read his books over and over. He helps me drink from the fountain of God's love.

Certain psalms are other places to find God's love. Psalm 45 gets me in touch with Him.

Some folks have not expanded their capacity for love in years. They have not increased their ability to give or receive love. To those dear people I want to say that there is not going to be an increase unless you drink more from the fountain of the love of God. You have to find a way to put yourself near that fountain so that you have a heart of love every day.

After you have experienced and demonstrated such love, you help encourage it in your leadership team, both with professional staff and lay leaders. In leadership settings, you can get candid about a spirit of love. Then when you are in leadership meetings where someone starts pointing the finger and saying, "I think that is a lousy idea," you can say, "Whoa, let's slow down and show more love. Let's back up. Let's go back to the basics here. Then we can call each other into account about love."

The starting point for deepening your spirit of love is to keep close to the fountain of God's love.

Fellowship with a Loving Group

Another way to expand your capacity for giving and receiving love is to fellowship with a small group who will show you love and expand your ability to be more loving. Hang around the most loving people you can find. Did you ever notice that after you have had a meal with extraordinarily loving people, you walk away with a hunger in your spirit that says, "I'd like to be a little more loving like them"?

Identify the most loving people you know, and get with them more. I have those people identified in my life. Then when I am with them, I ask them questions like, How did your heart get into expressing love? Who loved you so much? Was it a parent? Was it an aunt or an uncle? I know it is God, but what other factors helped you develop such an extraordinary capacity for loving and receiving love? How did you get it? How do you keep it?

Fascinating conversations often develop. One of my friends told me about her extraordinary, loving dad. In addition to the Heavenly Father, her earthly dad filled this woman's heart with love throughout her growing-up years. Once she explained, "I walk around knowing that I had two fathers who were crazy about me. So I felt loved all the time. That gives me the capacity to love others." Identify extraordinary, loving people in your life, and spend enough time with them that some of their loving perspectives and affirming ways rub off on you.

Pray to Be More Loving

Try making your desire for an expanded capacity for love a focus of your prayer. The idea is to ask God to give you more love and to make you more loving. If we could check everybody's prayer journal, we would likely find many requests for more comfort to come their way, for problems to be solved, or for God to get them out of a problem. But I urge you to purposely pray for more love.

Try praying on a regular basis for the fruit of the Spirit to increase in your life, especially love. I pray every day for an increased capacity to give and receive love. I have learned that if I spend time each day with that prayer focus, it affects me so I am more loving throughout the entire day. The fruit of the Spirit listed in Gal. 5:22-23 helps me keep my prayers focused: "Love, joy, peace, patience, kindness, goodness, faithfulness, gentleness and self-control." What a list.

My love capacity also increases when I sing the prayer, "More love to Thee, O Christ, / More love to Thee!" (Elizabeth Prentiss).

INTENTIONALLY CONFRONT "OUCH" SITUATIONS

Confrontation may seem a little risky, and it is. But in circles where the relationships are close and sometimes stressed—like a church staff—try this on a one-on-one individual basis for an extended period, maybe a whole afternoon. View it as an opportunity to get to know the individual better—his or her concerns, cares, and victories. Include questions in your discussion like, "What are the circumstances when I am most likely to hurt you or when you are the most likely to hurt me?"

In other words, what do we do that is most likely to make each other say, "Ouch"? I sometimes say to a staff member, "What are the attitudes and behaviors I exhibit that make you think 'Ouch, that hurt me'?" Such an awareness almost always increases love, opens communication, and strengthens relationships.

In such a setting, a member of our management team once said to me, "Your capacity to love goes up or down on the basis of how your weekend message is coming. So if I need to see you, I call your administrative assistant to find out how your message is coming. If she says pretty good, I come up. If she says it is slow, I stay away."

What an indictment that was for me.

Loving confrontation works the other way too. One management team member sometimes gives me an ouch with his sarcastic sense of humor. Though it is supposed to be good humor, I often feel the barb. That individual has no awareness of this problem, but he needs to know so he can increase his capacity to give and receive love.

Talking about these ouch factors helps everyone improve, and as a result, bold love increases in your staff and church. But it is not likely to happen without a specific and safe plan being developed where it is safe to speak about ouch factors. And the leader must take the lead to foster such a climate of openness, trust, and acceptance.

Learn to Express Love

You probably know how difficult this challenge can be from personal experience. Many of us feel love for others but do not feel comfortable or know how to express these feelings. One of my goals is to help people get their love out of their hearts into someone else's heart. To do that, I always start with myself.

Some of us think when we feel love for a family member or a ministry team member, "I ought to express this love," or "I ought to do some loving deed." But for some mysterious reason, an automatic editing process takes place inside us, so our good intention gets choked off, and our voice is mute.

Why Does It Seem Risky?

"I am not going to do that," you might reason. "I might express it wrongly. I might cause a misunderstanding. I might create a monster I'm going to have to feed." When we fall into this skewed pattern of thinking, let's ask ourselves an important question: Does expressed love ever hurt anybody? Of course, the answer is no.

For the longest time when I got serious about being able to give and receive love, I felt the love of Christ for other people through me, but I was unwilling to take risks to express it. I came out of the Dutch Christian Reformed subculture, where the idea was "buck up." The unexpressed communication taught us, "Let's not get touchy-feely, nurturing, and all that stuff. We've got a job to do." Many of us grew up in homes and churches like that, so we feel emotionally tongue-tied and unresponsive.

I was so confused about expressing love that I actually convinced myself if I felt love for another person, that was about the same as expressing it. Let's get realistic. If you feel love and do not express it, the other person is still walking around not knowing how you feel. He or she gains no benefit from unexpressed love.

Follow the Pattern of Jesus

While studying the way Jesus expressed love, I finally crossed a line in my life. I said to myself, "I'm tired of not expressing love. I have to change." At that point, I concluded, "I can no longer blame my background. I cannot blame my church. I cannot blame my family. This is my life. This is my spouse. These are my children. These are my friends. This is my staff. This is my church. I have to take responsibility for what I am doing with the unexpressed love I feel for them in my heart."

So I started to say, "I love you."

I felt like an absolute fool the first few times I did it. I felt uncomfortable and strange. To say to our finance officer, "Hey, I really love you, and I'm glad you are on our team." Or to say to a woman, who has been one of our elders for 20 years, "I love you. You are a sister in Christ, and I think about you in loving, sisterly ways. I want the best for you, and I pray for you."

But the freedom this has brought! Now it is a regular part of my vocabulary. I am proud my kids are comfortable with that now. Every phone call, every time Todd or Shauna goes out the door, "Love you, Dad." I answer, "Love you, kiddo." "Love you, Bud." Every time.

Sooner or later, you must decide if you are going to be an expresser of bold love. You must decide if you are going to deprive other people of the gift of the love of Christ you feel for them. Or are you going to take the plunge and increase the joy you give and the satisfaction you feel?

CROSS THE LINE AT A DEFINING MOMENT

So much of life is determined by decision points. We call them defining moments. I lived on the limiting side of love for a long time, but I finally stepped over to the other side.

I want to challenge you to walk across that line, too, so when you see your wife, husband, son, daughter, or team member, you say, "I love you." You will be amazed at what that does. The whole atmosphere around you will change.

Many people comment on the loving atmosphere around Willow Creek Community Church. It is not an accident. Neither is it an aroma that comes and goes. It has taken years of helping people grow in their capacity to drink from the fountain of the love of God and then challenging them to speak of that love to each other. In this process, we have even learned it is hard to get ugly at an elders' meeting when we start by spending time building community by saying "I love you" to each other.

THE POWER OF A NOTE

I also need to express love and affirmation in writing. Some of us are auditory, so when we hear "I love you," it is settled and done. But others need something in their hands so they can look at it again and again. I so much love to get notes and letters that I have a desk drawer dedicated for keeping such notes. Then when I need encouragement, I pull them out of my desk and reread them.

The power of a love note is incredible. A couple of years ago, we were doing a training conference in Hamburg, Germany. My daughter, Shauna, was studying at the time in London. Since we had not seen each other for quite a while, I flew her over to Hamburg for a dinner and a part of the conference. She stayed overnight in the hotel with me but had to leave the next day to go back to school. When I got back in my room after she left, I found this note on the pillow: "Dad, I love you so much. This is one more of the many memories we share together. Thank you, I am proud to be your daughter. There are many people at this conference that are thankful for you and owe much to you, but no one more than I. I pray for you, and I will pray for the team for the rest of this trip." It was signed, "Your Daughter."

What kind of gift is a note like that to a dad? What kind of gift is it to a daughter when you write a note back? What kind of gift is a similar note to a spouse? What kind of gift to a staff person or lay church member?

Enjoying the Journey

Of course, we all have hills to climb and a world to win. But the time has come to cross the line of silence. It's time to say we are no longer willing to sacrifice togetherness and community on the altar of a great cause. We need to tell ourselves if there cannot be heart and love in the efforts, we do not want to take the hills anymore. If we cannot be a loving group of people enjoying the journey and giving each other love along the way, then the work is too hard and the accomplishments are too hollow. Without love, ministry gets too mechanical and shrinks our hearts in the process.

Touch Those You Love

The power of touch comes from Scripture. Jesus was the master at giving an appropriate, loving touch. He wanted to convey love to kids, so instead of waving at them, He would stop. He would hold them in His lap and touch them.

Though Jesus had the power to do drive-by healings, He didn't. He touched people. He touched the eyes of a blind person. He touched a leper who had seldom been touched. He showed that massive amounts of love could be conveyed through an appropriate touch. A hand on the shoulder, a handshake, or a friendly hug often makes an incredible impact on another person.

I was leading a staff retreat when I asked the group to each think of an unforgettable childhood experience he or she could share. One great big guy stood up and said his most important childhood memory was riding in the front seat of the family car with his mom and dad on vacation. He said, "I remember it so vividly because my mom would be stroking my leg and my dad would pull me under his arm. Life just did not get better than that."

A brief, appropriate touch can convey a lot of love. Of course, you know the boundaries between an encouraging and a sensual touch. Some of us are paranoid about that. I am not a big hugger, especially with strangers. But let's remember that a loving, appropriate touch can communicate a lot of love.

Do Small Acts of Kindness

This one is fairly easy. Scripture says in Eph. 4:32, "Be kind and compassionate to one another"; and in 1 John 3:18, "Let us not love with words or tongue but with actions and in truth." I was on an around-the-world speaking tour, and it was a rough trip. When I came back, I landed past midnight.

Lynne picked me up at O'Hare. Though I always go in through the garage door, she said, "You must go in the front door of the house tonight."

I said, "Not now."

She said, "Trust me; go in the front door."

I went in the front door, and she said, "We have to go wake up Todd."

I said, "Let's let him sleep."

She replied, "No, no."

So we woke Todd. He sprang out of bed and said, "Oh, man! I've got something to show you, Dad."

He took me out to the garage. While I was gone, he had painted the garage walls, hung some pictures, and installed part of his sound system. He knows I like to wash my car and hang out in the garage. He had redone our garage as a gift to me. When I told him I was deeply touched by his gift, Todd replied, "Dad, it just took me a couple of half days. It's a little thing."

"Todd, every time I pull in this garage, I will think of a son who did such a loving thing for me," I said.

Think about it. You know many small kindnesses that would gladden the hearts of people close to you. You know their recreations. You know the kind of things staff members love to do. You know what would be special to your kids. It only takes a few minutes to be thoughtful and take action so you can say, "During my day I was thinking about you. So here is what I did."

CARRY OTHERS' BURDENS AND ENJOY THEIR VICTORIES

This means entering into the joys and sorrows of those around us. This one comes right out of Scripture: "Rejoice with those who rejoice; mourn with those who mourn" (Rom. 12:15).

I do not know of anything that more closely bonds hearts than someone who says, "I would not think of missing this party. I will be the first one to celebrate with you. I would not think of not being a part of your great victory."

The same is true of sorrows and pain. At Willow Creek, we were about four days away from Easter and behind in our preparations. Then our drama director's mother passed away unexpectedly, and the funeral was to be held in Minneapolis. The programming team felt terrible that they could not attend the funeral.

The leader came into my office the day after the mother's death and said, "This is not good. I understand that we have to do our Good Friday and Easter services. But it is a violation of community for us not to be with Steve at his mother's funeral."

"Let me make a couple of phone calls."

I called several board members and said, "Could we allocate some money to charter a small airplane to get our folks up there to attend the funeral and come right back so that we can do the work?" It was a short conversation, because the board members said, "Absolutely!"

We charted a twin-engine aircraft, and the team went up there, helped Steve bury his mom, flew back, and went to work. To this day, when Steve writes me notes sometimes, he says, "I know the heart of this church was to make sure I wouldn't be alone in that situation." I do not know if it is the heart of this church or the heart of Christ. But as members of the Body of Christ, we rejoice and weep with each other. We do the mountains and the valleys together.

In the early days of the church, when my dad died over in Michigan, scores and scores of people made the 165-mile drive to stand with me. You remember those things the rest of your life.

MAKE YOUR CHURCH A COMMUNITY OF BOLD LOVE

Let me paint a beautiful picture for you. Can you imagine what would happen if every leader in your church took personal responsibility to regularly drink from the fountain of the love of God? To regularly interact with loving people who could grow their heart and would pray every day, "God, increase my capacity to give and receive love"? Can you imagine if every leader in your church would double his or her capacity to give and receive bold love? Can you imagine what would happen if people whose hearts are full of Christ were saying loving things and writing loving things to each other? Can you imagine the impact if your church members offered each other appropriate, loving touches, did acts of kindness, and freely entered into each others' joys and sorrows? What kind of churches would we lead!

Bold love is not going to cost more money. You do not have to attend more conferences to begin. You do not have to negotiate or legislate. Just start. If you create loving communities like the one I have described, first-time seekers will sniff it and say, "I want in." Crusty old veteran believers whose hearts have shut down will warm up again. Arrogant people will have their pride melted.

Love changes people. Love transforms churches. Love is the greatest force in the world and the most needed component in contemporary churches.

Start the love revolution in your congregation today.

This chapter is reprinted from *Making Church Relevant* in the Beeson Pastoral Series, Dale Galloway, comp. (Kansas City: Beacon Hill Press of Kansas City, 1999), 45-58. Reprinted by permission of Bill Hybels.